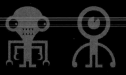

Are We Alone?

Scientists Search for Life in Space

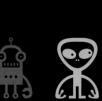

by Gloria Skurzynski

NATIONAL GEOGRAPHIC
WASHINGTON, D.C.

My deepest thanks go to Ed, as always. Without you, it wouldn't happen.
This book is dedicated to Seth Shostak, Jill Tarter, Nathalie Cabrol, David Des Marais, and all the
generous scientists in these pages who shared their time and expertise to help the author.
(Though their titles are not mentioned, all the scientists are Ph.D.s)   G.S.

Library of Congress Cataloging-in-Publication Data
Skurzynski, Gloria.
  Are we alone? : scientists search for life in space / by Gloria
    Skurzynski.
    v. cm.
    ISBN: 0-7922-6567-X
  Contents: Flying saucers—Extraterrestrial civilizations—
    Telescopes—Nodding at midnight—A better way to
    look—The quest—It's elemental—One extreme to
    another—From earth to mars—Jupiter's icy moons—
    Talking to E.T.I. 1. Life on other planets—Juvenile litera-
    ture. 2. Milky Way—Juvenile literature. [1. Life on other
    planets. 2. Milky Way.] I. Title.
  QB54.S584 2004
  576.8'39—dc22
                      2003017732

Published by the National Geographic Society
John M. Fahey, Jr., President and Chief Executive Officer
Gilbert M. Grosvenor, Chairman of the Board
Nina D. Hoffman, Executive Vice President, President of
  Books and Education Publishing Group
Ericka Markman, Senior Vice President, President, Children's
  Books and Education Publishing Group

STAFF FOR THIS BOOK:
Nancy Laties Feresten, Vice President, Editor-in-Chief,
  Children's Books, Project Editor
Bea Jackson, Art Director, Children's Books
Bea Jackson and Dan Sherman, Designers
Janet Dustin, Illustrations Coordinator
Connie D. Binder, Indexer
R. Gary Colbert, Production Director
Lewis R. Bassford, Production Manager
Vincent P. Ryan, Manufacturing Manager

PHOTO CREDITS: iv—1: Seth Shostak; 2: University of Colorado
Board of Regents with thanks to Jim Giglio and Bob Keefer: 4: Mark
Meyer; 5: Mitch Mascaro/The Herald Journal; 8: FOTOSearch/
Image State; 12: Photo Courtesy of the National Astronomy and
Ionosphere Center, Arecibo Observatory, a facility of the National
Science Foundation, photo by David Parker; 15: Seth Shostak; 18:
Art by Holly Warburton; 20: John Gleason and Steve Mandel; 23:
© the SETI League, Inc. Used by permission.; 26: Ed Skurzynski;
28: Ly Ly, SETI Institute; 31: National Radio Astronomy
Observatory/AUI; 32: David Aguilar; 35: Ed Skurzynski; 38: Akira
Fuji, Courtesy of NASA/JPL; 40: Courtesy of NASA/JPL; 41:
Courtesy of Ray Jayawardhana; 42: NASA and A. Schaller; 44:
Roger Lynds, National Optical Astronomy Observatory/AURA/
NSF/WIYN; 47: Ed Skurzynski; 51: Robert Finkbeiner; 53:
Courtesy of the Smithsonian, artist Peter Sawyer; 54: David Des
Marais; 56: CORBIS; 58: Image courtesy of John C. Priscu,
Montana State University at Bozeman; 59: Photo by Rocco
Mancinelli; 62: David A. Doudna, WC&PRURC; 64: © Woods Hole
Oceanographic Institution; 68: Brian Grigsby; 71: Ed Skurzynski;
74: Art by Attila Hejja; 75: Courtesy of NASA/JPL; 78: Paul
Schenk/LPI; 81: Taylor Bucci; 82: Courtesy of NASA/JPL; 84:
Cornell University News Service; 85: Ed Skurzynski; 88: Lauren
Thliveris.

One of the world's largest nonprofit scientific and educational organizations, the National Geographic Society was founded in
1888 "for the increase and diffusion of geographic knowledge." Fulfilling this mission, the Society educates and inspires millions every day through its magazines, books, television programs, videos, maps and atlases, research grants, the National
Geographic Bee, teacher workshops, and innovative classroom materials. The Society is supported through membership dues,
charitable gifts, and income from the sale of its educational products. This support is vital to National Geographic's mission
to increase global understanding and promote conservation of our planet through exploration, research, and education.

For more information, please call 1-800-NGS LINE (647-5463) or write to the following address:

NATIONAL GEOGRAPHIC SOCIETY
1145 17th Street N.W., Washington, D.C. 20036-4688 U.S.A.
Visit the Society's Web site at www.nationalgeographic.com.

TABLE OF CONTENTS

Is Anybody Out There?

IT'S THE MIDDLE OF MARCH. Here in the tropics, March does not come in like a lion—the evening is warm and calm. As the Sun sets behind the hills, it casts shadows across an immense aluminum bowl sunk in the ground. This bowl is the reflector of a telescope, the largest, most sensitive single-dish radio telescope in the world. Located near the city of Arecibo in Puerto Rico, it is called the Arecibo Observatory.

One thousand feet in diameter, the dish is too large to move around and point at particular patches of sky. But suspended high above it is the Gregorian feed, a 75-ton dome that holds two smaller reflectors and a receiver, and this dome does move. Although its two mirrors are focused on the darkening sky, they don't see anything. This is not an optical telescope that picks up images of stars and planets in its lenses—it's a radio telescope that collects radio signals from nearby Sunlike stars.

Astronomer Peter Backus walks from a trailer into a building that overlooks the bowl. Heading along a corridor past rooms full of complex electronic equipment, Peter reaches a control room where fellow astronomer Seth Shostak sits peering at a computer screen. Other tables in the room hold several additional computers. This March evening, Seth and Peter are observing for Project Phoenix, which is part of the SETI Institute. SETI stands for Search for Extraterrestrial Intelligence. Not just for E.T.s (Extraterrestrials), but for E.T. Intelligence.

Hovering above the giant dish, the Gregorian dome's reflectors catch and focus weak radio waves.

CHAPTER ONE

Flying Saucers

One of the meanings of the word "extra" is "beyond." *Terrestrial* is from the Latin word for Earth. Put them together—*extraterrestrial*—and you have "beyond Earth." Extraterrestrial life might be found within our solar system, beyond it in our Milky Way galaxy, or even farther out in the universe.

Acccording to polls, half the people on Earth believe that intelligent, nonhuman beings exist somewhere "out there." Thousands say they have spotted alien spacecraft hovering in our skies. Others say they have actually seen extraterrestrial beings—or even been kidnapped by them and taken into their space ships. These alien ships are called UFOs, or unidentified flying objects.

One of the first reported UFO incidents happened on June 24, 1947, when a pilot named Kenneth Arnold flew his private airplane from Washington State to his home in Boise, Idaho. During the flight, just before three o'clock in the afternoon, Mr. Arnold saw nine mysterious

Would you be convinced by this picture of UFOs? It's from a 1947 Brazilian newspaper. They really aren't UFOs; they're lenticular clouds.

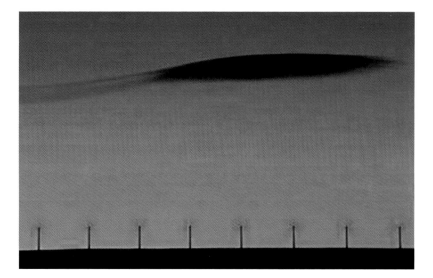

crescent-shaped objects traveling incredibly fast near the Cascade mountain range. He said they moved like a saucer would if you skipped it over water.

When Arnold landed in Pendleton, Oregon, to refuel his plane, he told his story to the editor of the local newspaper, who published it. Mr. Arnold didn't say the mysterious objects *looked* like saucers; he said they *moved* like saucers. But his story was picked up by a number of newspapers, and within a month the term "flying saucers" had found its way into people's vocabularies. Soon flying saucers supposedly were being seen everywhere, not just in the United States, but all over the world. People were sure these flying saucers had come from outer space, brought here by extraterrestrials who were spying on us or who wanted something we Earthlings had that the aliens didn't possess on their own planets. It all started because Kenneth Arnold used the words "moved like a saucer would if you skipped it over water."

What did Kenneth Arnold actually see? Possibilities

Two men never quite admitted to making these crop circles in Utah, but one of them, named Mike, left his signature in the field. Can you find it?

range from a flock of geese to airplane lights to a meteor shower, plus a lot of other guesses. The U.S. Air Force investigated and reported that it might have been a mirage, or that he may have seen lenticular clouds, which are formed when strong winds blow over high mountains. (Lenticular clouds are often saucer shaped.)

Scientists tried to explain that lots of natural phenomena appear in our skies and some could be mistaken for flying saucers. There are Leonid smoke rings, which are sometimes visible after a meteor shower, and there are Venus pillars—shafts of light that jut out from the top and bottom of Venus, a planet easy to spot. In recent years, added to the tricks Nature can play are our own satellites and space debris. When space hardware drops out of orbit to crash toward Earth, it usually breaks into chunks that can glow from the sun's reflection or from the heat of reentry, and can leave contrails like an airplane's. To someone on the ground or in an airplane, these glowing fragments might look like a whole fleet of alien invaders.

In 1947, just weeks after the Arnold sighting, a UFO allegedly crashed north of Roswell, New Mexico. Several Roswell citizens reported hearing an explosion and then discovering debris scattered over surrounding fields. Officers at the nearby Roswell Army Air Base announced that what people thought was a UFO was nothing more than a weather balloon and that so-called alien bodies were just crash dummies being tested in the balloon. Nevertheless, the Roswell Incident, as it became known, convinced even more people that extraterrestrials had come to visit Earth.

Believers

In the 1970s, a new type of alien signal was reported. Circles, both simple and complex in design, began to appear in fields of grass, wheat, or barley. They came in all sizes, ranging from a few yards across to a mile wide. Believers in extraterrestrials felt sure the crop circles were messages sent to Earth by aliens. Much later, in 1991, two elderly Englishmen confessed they'd sculpted hundreds of these crop circles as a hoax.

True believers scoffed that the men's confessions themselves were a hoax, simply a plot hatched by the British Ministry of Defense and the American CIA to conceal the truth, just as they'd covered up facts about Roswell and other flying saucer events. Today a majority of people, including 72 percent of Americans, say they think UFOs are real and that world governments are hiding evidence about them.

In at least one case, the British government actually did keep secret files. Below is a report written by the American deputy base commander at Woodbridge Royal Air Force Base in eastern England in 1980.

TO: RAF/CC

1. Early in the morning of 27 DEC 80 (approximately 0300), two USAF security police patrolmen saw unusual lights outside the back gate at RAF Woodbridge. Thinking an aircraft might have crashed or been forced down, they called for permission to go outside the gate to investigate. The on-duty flight chief responded and allowed three patrolmen to proceed on foot. The individuals reported seeing a strange glowing object in the forest. The object was described as being metallic in appearance and triangular in shape, approximately two to three meters across the base and approximately two meters high. It illuminated the entire forest with a white light. The object itself had a pulsing red light on top and a bank(s) of blue lights underneath. The object was hovering or on legs. As the patrolmen approached the object, it maneuvered through the trees and disappeared. At this time the animals on the nearby farm went into a frenzy. The object was briefly sighted approximately an hour later near the back gate.

CHARLES I. HALT, Lt. Col. USAF

Deputy Base Commander

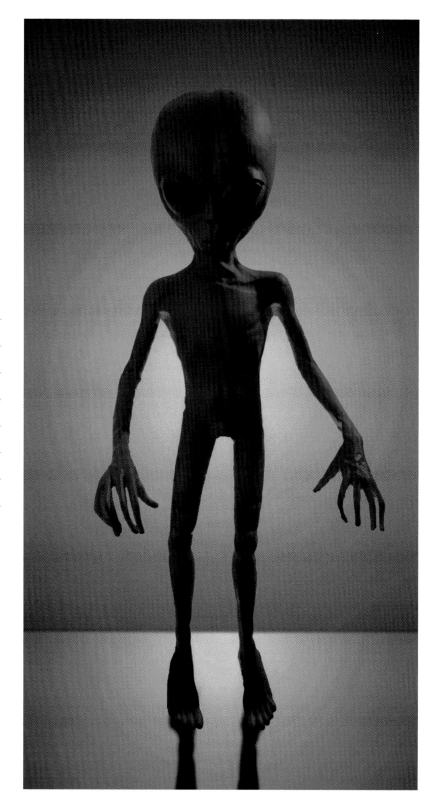

Believers say extraterrestrial visitors look like this. Movie producer and director Steven Spielberg may have started it all with *Close Encounters of the Third Kind* and *E.T.—the Extraterrestrial.*

That sounds so convincing, how could anyone doubt that it really happened? But when you think about the highly detailed report, you may begin to ask questions. For instance, why didn't anyone take pictures? Well, they did, the airmen said, but the pictures didn't turn out because something was wrong with the film. Does that mean that at an air force base with hundreds of people living on the base or near it, *no one* had a camera with good film? And no one bothered to phone a TV station? If they had, TV reporters and cameramen would have swarmed all over the scene as fast as their cars could get them there.

Another cause for doubt: Woodbridge Royal Air Force base had a radar system. Yet the British Ministry of Defense reported, "No unidentified object was seen on radar during the period in question, and there was no evidence of anything having intruded into UK [British] airspace and landed near RAF Woodbridge." The official government report, called the Rendlesham File, was released at the end of 2002 under the Freedom of Information Act. It suggests that the unusual lights were probably beams from a nearby lighthouse.

Movies have encouraged people to believe in extra-terrestrials. *Close Encounters of the Third Kind* (1977) showed space aliens with big heads, large tilted eyes, and childlike bodies. Those E.T.s were not warlike; they just wanted to study humans. In the movie *E.T.* (1982 and 2002), the visitor from outer space was not only non-threatening, he was scared of people! He looked a bit like the aliens in *Close Encounters* (maybe because Steven

Spielberg worked on both films). Most movie aliens have hands with fewer than five digits, big eyes, and smooth skin that varies in color from silver to white to pale gray. (Believers in extraterrestrials call them the Grays.) Just as the term "flying saucer" stuck in people's minds, those big-headed, spindly-bodied creatures took hold of the popular imagination. Even people who claim actually to have met aliens describe them the same way. Is that art imitating life or believers being influenced by the films they see?

No one has ever managed to photograph an actual alien, but photos of flying saucers do appear every now and then in the press or on the Internet. Yet in this age of high-quality cameras—film, digital, and video—the saucer images always look fuzzy or smeared. The few sharp and detailed photos of alien spaceships have been proved to be fakes, snapshots taken of a Frisbee hurled into the air, or altered by a computer whiz for fun or for profit.

Unbelievers

Do serious scientists believe these reports of UFO sightings and alien visitors to Earth? The answer is no. Scientists demand proof before they'll believe in anything at all. There has never been any proof that visitors from beyond Earth have hovered over our planet, or have carved fields of corn or wheat into designs, or have taken humans into their spaceships and then returned them. There's been no hard evidence, not a single artifact left behind—a lost boot, a shred of whatever material the UFO was made of, or even a flake of alien skin. Without any kind of physical evidence, people's stories about alien sightings and encounters can't be verified.

Scientists have a logical argument against alien visits: The distance between Earth and the star nearest to our own Sun is more than four light-years. That's about 24 trillion (24,000,000,000,000) miles. If the aliens have a rocket technology at the same stage of development as ours is, it would take several hundred thousand years to make the trip—that is, if there were no stops en route and no catastrophic collisions with space debris. But why would they want to spend enormous time and wealth and energy resources to fly past *us*?

Nevertheless, although scientists don't think aliens have ever visited Earth, that doesn't mean they doubt their existence. Somewhere beyond our galaxy, an advanced technological civilization or two might be leaking radio signals, intentionally or otherwise. Back at Arecibo, in a small room on a tropical island that often gets swept by hurricanes, Seth Shostak and Peter Backus stare hopefully at wiggly lines on small screens, trying to find *proof* that E.T.s do exist.

CHAPTER TWO

Extraterrestrial Civilizations

Peter and Seth wait and hope for a signal from outer space—not the random radio static emitted by the gas between stars or by energetic galaxies, not the rapid beat of a pulsar, but a deliberate signal sent by technologically savvy creatures somewhere beyond Earth.

Transmissions from an advanced civilization, if one exists, would spread in waves from their planet or moon or asteroid, just as transmissions have been leaking away from our own planet Earth since radio and television first began to broadcast. By now, Earthly TV leaks have traveled outward for 64 light-years. If any of the 1,500 stars they've rippled past have planets with television sets, alien inhabitants might be watching the original *Mickey Mouse Club*.

Twice a year since 1998, Project Phoenix astronomers have been coming to the large radio telescope at Arecibo. Project Phoenix examines individual stars rather than scanning the whole sky, because, according to Peter, "In a vast sky full of stars, only a fraction are likely to have

The Arecibo Observatory in Puerto Rico is part of the National Astronomy and Ionosphere Center. It operates 24 hours a day, every day.

life-supporting planets and be near enough for us to detect radio waves transmitted at a reasonable power." On this March night they've observed stars HD 140913, HD 157214, HD 163840, and many others. Very few stars have names such as "Betelgeuse." Most have only an ID number.

As the 75-ton Gregorian dome changes its position above the big dish, radio waves make the electrons in the Gregorian dome's receivers vibrate faster, producing electrical currents that travel down cables to the control room. The currents are translated into zigzag lines the astronomers watch on the computer screens.

Some of the lines wiggle sideways on the screen, some spike up and down. Other signals look like the "snow" you see on your television set when you turn to a channel that isn't broadcasting. Here in the control room, for 40 nights a year from dusk to dawn, scientists hope, observe, and wait for that one alien signal to light up their screens. What keeps them going?

Numbers. Enormous numbers.

Starting small, begin with the number one. That's how many planets we know are home to intelligent life—our own planet, Earth. Go to nine, the number of planets in our solar system. Does life exist on any of those other planets? Possibly, but if so, it is not intelligent life capable of sending messages to Earth. A hundred years ago, some scientists thought that smart Martians were building canals to irrigate the red soil. Those scientists were mistaken.

Now the numbers explode. Our sun is one of 100 billion stars, more or less, in our Milky Way galaxy. The

Milky Way is a billion billion kilometers, or 120,000 light-years, in diameter. (One light-year is 5,878,786,100,000 miles—almost 6 trillion.) Beyond our own galaxy are at least 100 billion other galaxies, maybe as many as 400 billion. That calculates to about 10,000 million million million stars—or more—in the universe.

It has already been proved that some of those stars have planets orbiting them. More than 120 planets have been discovered so far, and additional ones are being found regularly as astronomers study our galaxy. It would be illogical to assume that Earth is the only planet that supports life of any kind.

Add "intelligent" to "life," and the certainty declines, but the sheer number of probable planets is still large. Add "civilizations with advanced technology," and the number drops further. To that add "civilizations that transmit radio signals," and it becomes a real guessing game. Still, the possibility looks good.

How the Search Began

A scientist named Frank Drake liked the odds. According to Frank, the question of whether intelligent life exists in space had been left too long to science fiction writers. "Our technology has advanced to the state," he said, "where these questions can no longer be ignored by the scientists." This was back in 1960.

In April of that year, Frank conducted the first ever radio search for extraterrestrial intelligence. At Green Bank, West Virginia, using an 85-foot radio telescope, he began to observe two nearby stars. "We started tuning these fancy receivers at about 4 a.m.," he remembers. "The receivers were new and very temperamental, and they took about an hour of complicated tuning to make them work the way we needed them to. Only two people in the world knew how to do it, the engineer who built them and myself."

Right away they picked up a signal, a loud one. "We were very excited. We couldn't believe our luck," Frank said. The signal turned out not to be from extraterrestrials but from a secret military project. It was only the first of many similar disappointments over the next 40-some years.

Frank's experiment attracted attention, though, and other scientists became interested in the search, not just in the United States, but in Australia, Europe, and the Soviet Union (now a group of countries including Russia). Over the next four decades, radio telescope technology improved vastly. "Our equipment is 100 trillion times more powerful" than it was back in 1960, Frank says.

Yet Frank, along with hundreds of dedicated scientists and millions of citizens on Earth, is still waiting for that contact with another—what would we call it? Another race? No, we already use that term to classify people on Earth. Another species? No, we use that term too, to separate types of plants and animals. We've been using the words "aliens" and "extraterrestrials," but those are more about where the creatures come from than what they are. Maybe we should call them "technologists," since the one thing we'd know about them is that they're capable of building transmitters.

Imagining E.T.

Unless you're positive that E.T.s look like the Grays, you might try to build an image based on logic. For starters, don't expect them to look like you. If you go to the zoo you'll find creatures who do look something like you: the chimps and monkeys and gorillas. But you'll find hundreds more that don't resemble you at all, such as snakes and turtles and giraffes. In the aquarium are fish and dolphins and octopuses. All these Earthly specimens share the planet with you, have DNA very similar to yours, and have evolved over the same 3.5 billion years that produced you.

Now, think of intelligent aliens who have evolved on a different planet orbiting a different star. Life may have arisen on other planets in a completely different process than on Earth. We would still probably have some things in common, though. Any living creatures we find are likely to be made of hydrogen, nitrogen, carbon, and oxygen. All those elements are freely available in our galaxy.

We have no idea what
extraterrestrials, if there
are any, might look like,
but we know they won't
look anything like us.

If the aliens live on a planet with strong gravity, they may be built low to the ground. If the planet's gravity is weak, they could be tall and delicate. Either way, they'll need a skeletal system to support them.

If their planet doesn't have an atmosphere, the aliens' body covering may be thick and dark to prevent the damage caused by high ultraviolet radiation. If the planet has a thick atmosphere that blocks light, the organs of sight may be large in order to gather a lot of light. If the atmosphere is thin, their eyes could be slitted like a cat's to keep out glare. Atmosphere brings up the matter of lungs, or whatever feature the creatures use to breathe oxygen or any other gas their bodies need—that is, if they breathe at all.

They *will* need to eat, so they'll probably have some sort of mouth. Since they'll want to pick up things, they'll likely have appendages—one , two, three, or more hands on arms that are short or long or nonexistent. They'll need a method to move from place to place, but that doesn't mean they'll have feet. Perhaps their planet is mostly water, and they'll have fins that work on both solid and liquid surfaces. A central brainlike system will send and receive signals to and from all parts of the body, but the planet's engineers may have discovered ways to implant mechanical parts that increase intelligence and abilities, making the creatures into what we would call cyborgs.

In other words, we don't have a clue what they're going to look like. Still, if they're able to send radio signals throughout the galaxy, they'll belong to an advanced technological civilization.

CHAPTER THREE

Nodding at Midnight

Some areas of the galaxy are so clouded by gas and dust that they can't be seen with optical telescopes (the ones that capture visible light). But radio telescopes can penetrate those clouds to show what's beyond them. Since radio waves are longer than light waves, they have less energy and are easier to transmit. It also means they need a big area to be gathered into—the bigger the dish, the better to catch faint signals from interstellar space. That's why, compared with the mirrors in optical telescopes, radio antennas (the dishes) are huge. At 1,000 feet in diameter, the dish at Arecibo is the largest on Earth.

Big-dish radio telescopes are made of inexpensive metal. Arecibo's has aluminum panels perforated to let rain drip through onto the ground underneath so it won't collect in the dish, which actually looks pretty grimy when dirt blows in and plants grow up right through the panels.

Although radio telescopes have a lot of advantages, they have one big disadvantage, too: Radio waves are so

The universe is filled with gas and dust, making it hard to see details with optical telescopes. Other kinds of telescopes can penetrate the dust.

weak they could be drowned out by a cell phone on Jupiter, if there were such a thing as a cell phone on Jupiter. The hoped-for signal from an advanced E.T. civilization would undoubtedly be a faint one, with about a hundred million times less energy than a digital-watch battery. Here on Earth, radio signals are constantly drowned out by radar, by Global Positioning System (GPS) satellite signals, by televisions, and yes, by cell phone emissions. This means we might miss that important E.T. signal from space. Seth Shostak is hopeful, though. He says, "If an extraterrestrial broadcast breathes as much as 0.000000000000000000001 watts onto Arecibo's 18-acre reflector, we could detect it."

On this night, Peter and Seth have been observing for nearly six hours, and nothing exciting has happened. Three or four times the screens brightened with interesting signals, but they proved to be Earthly in origin. Project Phoenix astronomers observe frequencies that are between 1,000 megahertz and 3,000 megahertz. (Frequency means the number of times per second an electromagnetic wave (see glossary) passes a given point; a cycle is a wavelength; a hertz is one cycle per second; and a megahertz (abbreviated MHz) is a million cycles per second.) Before they first began to search, astronomers had to speculate on the frequency at which E.T.s would be most likely to transmit. The best possibility, because it's the quietest part of the spectrum, was thought to be about 1420 MHz. At that frequency there's not a lot of static from astronomical objects like galaxies or pulsars, so a faint E.T. signal should be easier to receive.

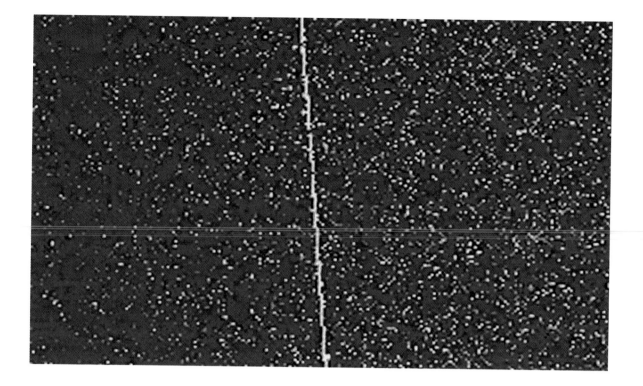

Every 0.7 second, Project Phoenix's signal-processing system measures 57.4 million channels. Each channel has a frequency 1 hertz wide. The data from a thousand of those channels make a line of dots across the top of the computer screen. In 1.4 seconds the next two lines appear on the screen, then the next appear and next and so on until the screen is filled and the bottom line is pushed off the screen by more lines coming in at the top. Whenever a notable signal comes in, its dots look brighter on the screen. As they collect they form a pattern. A signal means organized information; random noise is disorganized information. A straight up-and-down line indicates a steady signal that is likely to be Earthbound. A slanted line means the signal's frequency is drifting and might perhaps

This signal has never been identified, but it might have come from a global positioning system (GPS) satellite. Since no one knows the true source, it's called an anomaly.

be extraterrestrial. Both kinds of signals have been seen and checked on this March night by Seth and Peter.

False Alarm

At midnight, when their shift is over, Peter leaves, but Seth decides to stay for a few minutes to talk to Jill Tarter, the director of the Center for SETI Research at the SETI Institute. As the first in command, Jill could choose not to take the tiring shift from midnight till six a.m., but as she says, "Since it's the least favorite shift, the fact that the boss is willing to do it inspires the rest of the team to work a little harder." Arriving in the control room, she puts on a tape of her favorite samba music by a group called Viva Brazil. Others in the room stay seated and propel themselves on their wheeled office chairs from workstation to workstation, but Jill usually gets up and sambas across the floor.

After she is informed that nothing notable has happened between six and midnight, Jill reminisces with Seth about exciting signals that turned out to be false. "There was the night I was observing target 4505," Seth begins. Target 4505 is a Sunlike star that's 117 light-years away. Signals coming from the star had been checked by the System, as SETI people call the combination of computer programs and digital electronics that automatically checks all radio signals.

The guts of the System are stored in the trailer Peter visited earlier in the evening. The System keeps a list of known, human-created radio-interference patterns from telecommunications satellites, radar, television broadcasts, cell phones, and the hundreds of other sources that can interfere with a SETI observation. When a new signal arrives, it's checked against the list of already identified false signals.

"Target 4505 had passed all tests," Seth remembers. "We moved the telescope off the star system, and the signal went away. We ran it back on target, and the signal reappeared. It was looking good." The same procedure goes into effect whenever a promising signal occurs, and that happens as much as three or four times a night. If the new signal is not on the list of known interference, the System contacts the Lovell Telescope at Jodrell Bank, England, where other Project Phoenix team members are observing the skies. Because of Earth's rotation, an extraterrestrial signal would arrive at a slightly different frequency in England than in Puerto Rico.

If Jodrell Bank picks up the signal, the Arecibo telescope moves about 3 degrees distance from the target star. (That's about six times the diameter of the full moon.) The telescope at Jodrell Bank does the same thing. Both telescopes are checking to see whether the signal will disappear. It should, if it's really coming from that star. Next, the telescopes swing back to focus on the star again, to find out if the signal is still there. They call this procedure "nodding." Target 4505 passed this test, too.

Seth continues, "As target 4505 drifted out of sight to the west, I wrote in the log book, 'should be re-observed.' The next night, we did exactly that." This time the signal was seen not only in the direction of the star, but in other directions as well. It turned out to be just more Earthly interference, definitely not an extraterrestrial signal.

JILL TARTER

DIRECTOR OF THE CENTER

FOR SETI RESEARCH

SETI INSTITUTE

"When I was a little girl, every weekend my dad went hunting and fishing, and I went with him. I loved that time. My dad treated me like his son, the son he never had and always wanted, I guess. But I got to be about eight, and I suspect my mother and father had a conversation, because my dad sat me down and said, 'You know, you're getting to be a big girl. You probably ought to spend more time with your mother learning how to do girl things.' I burst into tears, I was so unhappy, and I just thought it was so unfair. Why did I have to either do what I did with my dad, or be a girl with my mom? My poor father—I must have really startled him. Tears, tears—huge unhappiness. And I said, 'Why can't I do both?' He said, 'I don't know. I guess you can. So what do you want to do?' I said, 'I want to be an engineer.'

"Why did I want to be an engineer? It was the most male thing I could think of. I didn't know what an engineer did, I didn't really know what the field of engineering was, but from that day on, I intended to be an engineer. Later, after I received my degree in engineering at Cornell, I took a course on star formation, and I decided, This is it. This is what I really want to do. And that's how I got hooked on astrophysics."

(Jill's father died when she was twelve years old. She misses him deeply.)

Jill has had her own false-alarm experiences. "Your first reaction," she says, "is not to believe it because you really want to be very diligent about doing all of the tests. So you try to disprove it. But as the signal stays around longer, like that time in Green Bank, West Virginia…." Her voice trails off as she remembers the incident at the 140-foot telescope at Green Bank, which is only a short distance from the antenna used by Frank Drake in 1960.

During that particular false alarm in 1997, the telescope was nodding back and forth between star and blank sky, and the signal appeared and disappeared. "It fooled us for so long because our second telescope had been struck by lightning and damaged," Jill says, shaking her head. "I even invented a new test for it. I ran the test, but although I'd written the software correctly, I was so excited that I misinterpreted the data. I got it wrong. We went through all this process, did the right things, did them correctly, and then when it came down to the final human interpretation, it got screwed up because I was too excited."

This was an incident that could not slip past unnoticed. Somehow, the news had already leaked. Within six hours, reporters from the *New York Times* called SETI to ask about the signal but had to be told there would be no earthshaking story for them to publish. If there had been, the news would have flashed instantly around the world.

Disappointments? Sure. But as Seth says, "We know that technology that's no more advanced than our own could send messages from star to star. Radio waves are fast and energetically cheap. We have the astronomy, and we have the technology. Our approach may not be the only approach, but it could work. Of that we're confident."

Ready to leave, Seth waves to Jill and heads outside, where the tropical night is filled with shrill chirps from frogs—both real and artificial. The imitation frog sounds are made by a device that indicates that the telescope is tracking. The real frogs, tiny ones known as *coquis*, have a two-tone call, and Seth jokes that they're "thumb-size frogs with watermelon-size throats." After all, it's a jungle out there, both surrounding the big dish and underneath it, where rapid tropical growth has to be cut back frequently so it won't reach up too far through the aluminum mesh of the dish.

Seth heads up the hill to the visiting scientists' quarters to catch some sleep. Soon, he and the other Project Phoenix astronomers will be saying goodnight to Arecibo—for good.

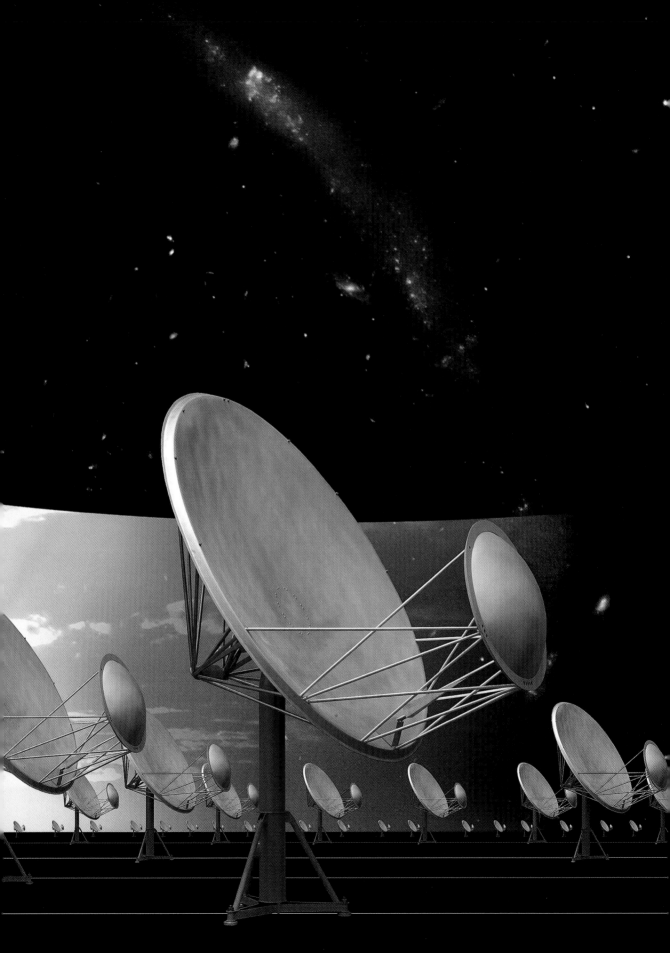

CHAPTER FOUR

A Better Way to Look

Each year, the Project Phoenix team has been able to use the Arecibo telescope only 5 percent of the time it operates. The other 95 percent of 'scope time goes to other scientists researching different projects.

All that is going to change. In 2005, Jill and Seth and Peter and the rest of their team will have their very own telescope, full-time, the fulfillment of a dream.

The dream actually began with a bitter blow in 1993. In 1992, on the 500th anniversary of Columbus's discovery of America, NASA had begun its own SETI project, but one year later, Congress refused to allow any further government funds to operate it. If SETI was going to survive at all, it had to rely on private donations. And it did survive, taking the name Project Phoenix from the bird in Greek mythology that dies in fire but is reborn in the ashes.

Fortunately, enough people believe in the value of searching for extraterrestrial intelligence that private funds have kept SETI operating, although its budget has been tight. One

Searching for signals from a technologically advanced civilization, the Allen Telescope Array (scheduled to be finished in 2005) may observe a million stars or more.

of SETI's biggest donors is Paul Allen, who made his fortune alongside Bill Gates at Microsoft. In the year 2000, Paul Allen donated $11.5 million to pay for the development of a new telescope that will be devoted nearly full-time to SETI.

Although another telescope the size of the one at Arecibo would cost about $100 million to construct at today's prices, there's a different way to build a large telescope that can study an even greater sky area, and it costs much less. When many small receiving dishes are combined side by side into what's known as an array, the dishes will work together like one large telescope. This is called interferometry, and the combination of dishes that all feed data into the same computer is called an interferometer.

In the beginning, the Allen Telescope Array (ATA) at Hat Creek, California, will consist of 350 aluminum dishes, each 20 feet in diameter. The radio waves these dishes gather will be combined in a central computer, making it seem that the waves were gathered by a single large dish rather than by 350 smaller ones. The ATA will cover frequencies between 0.5 and 11 GHz (a gigahertz is a billion cycles per second) and will have better resolution than the big dish at Arecibo.

"Constructing individual small antennas to serve as the pieces of a much larger radio mirror is not difficult," Jill Tarter says, "but connecting them all together to get them working is a major challenge."

The best part for the SETI team is that they'll be able to use the ATA for 24 hours a day, seven days a week, studying many different areas of the sky at the same time. That means that instead of a mere 1,000 stars, they'll be able to

The Very Long Baseline Array has ten radio antennas spread across the United States and its territories. It stretches from St. Croix in the Virgin Islands to Mauna Kea, Hawaii.

check out 100,000, or eventually as many as a million stars. Or more.

Other, bigger radio interferometers are already online. The Very Large Array in New Mexico can detect a golf-ball-size object a hundred miles away; the Very Long Baseline Array can measure the width of a human hair 250 miles distant and can spot something the size of a golf ball at the distance from New York to Los Angeles.

Radio astronomers have discovered pulsars and quasars and gamma-ray bursts and other celestial phenomena that were never imagined in past centuries, or even in the first part of the 20th century. And their combined 'scopes keep getting more powerful—or sensitive, as they prefer to say. When the Very Long Baseline Interferometer collects Earth-wide signals, it can pick out the *dimples* on a golf ball at the distance from New York to Los Angeles.

In the future, when interferometers get launched into space, the above claims will all seem rather primitive.

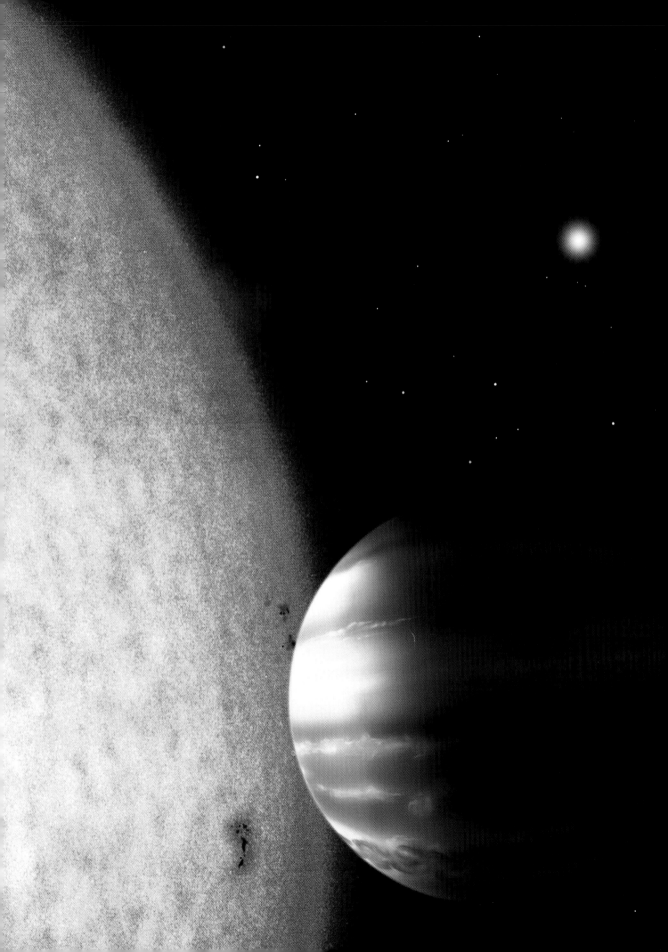

CHAPTER FIVE

The Quest

If there is life beyond our solar system, it's likely to be found on faraway planets. We already know these planets exist. The first extrasolar planet (meaning one in orbit around a star other than our sun) was found in 1995 by a team in Switzerland. Then early in 1996, Americans Paul Butler and Geoffrey Marcy announced that they'd discovered two more extrasolar planets.

Geoff and Paul detected their planets by what they call the "wobble" method. "Way back in 1985," Geoff remembers, "Paul Butler and I began sketching the idea for a new instrument, attached to a telescope, that might someday detect planets around other stars. Some very smart people told us that we wouldn't succeed, that we would never detect the wobble of a star caused by its attendant planets." Geoff and Paul tried anyway.

And they did succeed. Because of gravity, an orbiting planet will tug on its parent star just a little, pulling it toward the planet. If the star is being pulled toward Earth,

Astronomers haven't been able to actually see extrasolar planets—at least not so far—but they know they're out there orbiting distant stars in our Milky Way galaxy.

the slight motion will squeeze its light waves a minuscule amount, and when the planet goes around to the other side of the star, the light waves will lengthen the same slight amount. Geoff explains, "It's like watching a dog owner holding a leash without necessarily being able to see the dog. You watch how the owner's getting jerked around to determine how massive the dog is and what kind of path the dog is taking."

Geoff and Paul and other astronomers have applied another method to discover more planets. It's called the transit method. As Geoff describes it, "This transit method is very simple. The star is sitting there all by itself, shining with a constant amount of light, but if a planet crosses in front, the planet blocks a certain fraction of the light. It's just like when you have a lightbulb and a finger crosses in front of the lightbulb, the light from the bulb would dim due to the blocking of light by the finger." Called "brightness dips," these blockings are visible from Earth when Mercury or Venus crosses in front of our Sun.

The two planet-detection methods can work together. Using both the wobble method and the transit method, astronomers have found more than 120 extrasolar planets, and the number just keeps growing. (Geoff and Paul have discovered about two-thirds of them.) These newfound planets are quite different from the planets in our own solar system and are often as much as five to ten times more massive than our Jupiter. Many of them have eccentric, weirdly shaped orbits, sometimes quite close to their stars. One Jupiter-size planet whirls around its star every 29 hours. (Earth takes 365 days to travel around our Sun.)

"Clearly," Geoff says, "we're just seeing the tip of the planetary iceberg. We're seeing the biggest planets, the ones that are easiest to detect. But I have no doubt that there are smaller planets out there, yet to be detected, that our current technology simply can't find. So the real excitement is what we're going to do from here. Every time you point one of the giant Keck telescopes skyward, it feels like you're embarking on an epic voyage of discovery to explore the boundaries of the universe."

The Keck telescopes he's mentioning sit atop an extinct volcano called Mauna Kea on the Big Island of Hawaii. At an altitude of 13,800 feet (2,400 meters), the large optical and infrared telescopes named Keck I and Keck II stand above the clouds where the air is crisp and the skies are clear—about half the time. Unlike radio telescopes, which can collect signals through rain and clouds, optical telescopes gather light waves and become useless when the skies turn cloudy. If the stars aren't visible in the night sky, there's nothing to gather.

The twin Kecks combine to form the largest optical interferometer in the world. Mirrors at the two telescopes are each 33 feet wide, or more accurately 394 inches— they're called the 10-meter telescopes. The two white, domelike telescopes stand 275 feet (83.8 meters) apart on the mountaintop. An underground tunnel links them. In the tunnel the light waves from both Kecks are mixed and

GEOFFREY MARCY
PROFESSOR OF
ASTRONOMY
UNIVERSITY OF
CALIFORNIA AT BERKELEY

"When I was 14 years old, my mom and dad bought me a used telescope, a four-and-a-half-inch reflecting telescope. It was on wobbly legs, and the eyepiece mount barely worked, but I loved that telescope. I took it into my bedroom, and I tried to look at Saturn through the window, but the window made Saturn look blurry. So I took my window off. Then I pointed my telescope out the window and it worked much better, but I could only see a limited part of the sky. Next I took my telescope and went out through the hole in the wall onto the roof of a patio. That was perfect. I loved standing outside night after night watching the moons of Jupiter and the rings of Saturn—they just amazed me. I marked the position of Saturn's moon Titan night after night, just staying out on the patio roof. In summer in Los Angeles where I lived, it never rained. "

processed with a beam combiner and a camera to an exactness of one thousandth of a millimeter to create high-resolution images of heavenly bodies.

To Catch an Image

One of the astronomers who hopes for clear skies at Mauna Kea is Ray Jayawardhana. Ray was born in 1971 in Sri Lanka, an island nation south of India in the Indian Ocean. As a teenager, he found the skies fascinating. He taught himself English by reading astronomy books.

Now, on what has turned out to be a good night for observing Mauna Kea, Ray hopes to get really lucky and take a picture of a planet. That doesn't sound too extraordinary because ground-based telescopes and spacecraft have already photographed every planet in our solar system. But Ray wants to catch an image of an extrasolar planet—and that has never been done before.

Ray is already a star in the world of astronomy. At the age of 27, he photographed a star creating its own planets—at least that's what astronomers believe the image shows. Observing at a telescope in Chile in 1998, Ray focused on a star named HR 4796A and found a disk of dust around it. The disk was shaped like a flat doughnut, with empty space between the disk and its star. This is called a proto-planetary disk. In that empty space—the hole in the doughnut—dust grains are pulled together by gravity into boulder-size lumps that collide and combine until, in about a million years, they will form rocky planets like our Earth, Mercury, Venus, and Mars.

The Keck telescopes have been built to work as both optical and infrared telescopes, meaning they can detect both visible light and temperature. Everything in the universe that has a temperature above absolute zero (minus 460 degrees Fahrenheit, minus 273 degrees Celsius) emits some amount of heat, also called infrared radiation. Ray says, "The light from a star inside a cloud warms the dust around it. The dust then emits infrared light." The closer the dust grains are to a star, the higher their temperature will be. After the telescopes collect the infrared data, their computers analyze them and convert them into pictures called "false color" images, where colors are assigned to different wavelengths.

Goldilocks

"Imaging a Jupiter-like planet will be the first step to determining what its atmosphere is made of," Ray says. When scientists break the light from an object into its wave-lengths, they can tell what the object is made of and whether it might support life.

Scientists are pretty certain they know where a planet has to be to support life. It's called the "Goldilocks" zone—an orbit that's "not too cold, not too hot, but just right," which means it's not too close to its star's blazing heat but not too far away, either. That's just where our Earth happens to be: in a Goldilocks zone, more formally called a habitable zone.

Life, scientists believe, requires liquid water. A planet too far from its star would be so cold that whatever water it

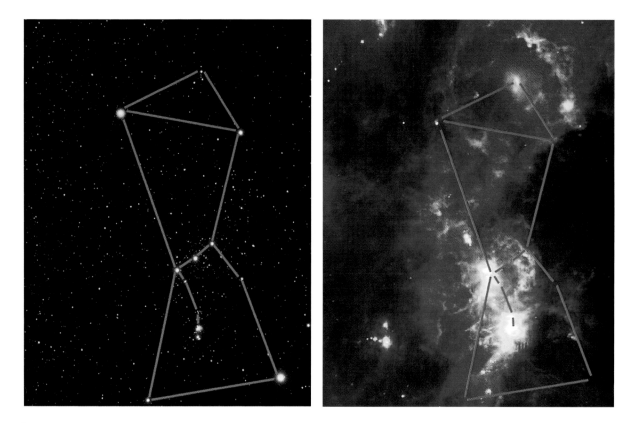

Optical telescopes detect visible wavelengths from the familiar stars that make up Orion (outlined in blue, left). Infrared telescopes reveal clouds of dust around and within the constellation (outlined in blue, right).

might have would be locked in a deep freeze forever. A planet too close to its star would be so hot that any water would have boiled away. The ideal Earthlike planet, on which life might flourish, would orbit just the right distance from its star for water to be liquid and to stay on the planet.

With all of the extrasolar planets discovered lately, the quest to take a picture of one keeps gathering momentum. "If you can take a picture of it, then you really know it's there," Ray says. "The first person to take a picture of one will owe a lot to luck and being in the right place at the right time with good weather." The race is "incredibly exciting because for the first time we have the technical capability to image an extrasolar planet. This is science on the frontier."

Going even farther onto the frontier, in the not too distant future there will be an even better way to search for extra-solar planets—not from Earth, but from space. The first attempt will be with a spacecraft called *Kepler*. *Kepler* will be devoted to finding Earthlike and larger planets in our Milky Way galaxy. Scheduled for launch sometime in 2007, the Kepler mission will use the transit method. Since it will search from orbit, Earth's atmosphere won't get in the way, so the view will be clearer and *Kepler* will be able to see smaller "brightness dips." Over a four-year period, *Kepler* will constantly scan 100,000 stars in a sky area equal to about two scoops of the Big Dipper.

Kepler is just the beginning. In the next several decades, if the U.S. Congress agrees to the funding, NASA plans to launch several amazingly sophisticated space telescopes to look for distant planets that may hold life. Here are some of the missions being planned:

The *Space Interferometry Mission* (SIM) is scheduled for launch in 2009, if all goes well. An optical interferometer, SIM will trail after Earth as it orbits the sun, like a puppy following its master. Using the wobble method, SIM will search for Earth-size planets in or near the habitable zones of 50 stars. But SIM is only the opening act for a much bigger and more far-seeing space interferometer to come.

Planned to launch between 2012 and 2015, the *Terrestrial Planet Finder* (TPF) will look for planets around stars—as many as 200 of them—up to 45 light-years away. Although the telescope designs aren't complete, TPF should be able to make images of planets as small as Earth.

TPF's instruments will detect heat emitted by any planets it discovers. Its onboard spectroscope will record the infrared or optical radiation that shows what the planet's surface is made of and whether it contains any "biosignatures."

Spectrometry spreads starlight into a rainbow of color. Each element in a star's atmosphere absorbs particular wavelengths of light that show up as lines on a spectrograph. The lines indicate various chemicals present in the planet's atmosphere, such as oxygen, carbon dioxide, methane, and more. Called absorption lines, they're like a fingerprint that identifies the molecules they came from. Finding liquid water, ozone, methane, and carbon dioxide all on one planet would be a biosignature like Earth's and would most likely mean the exoplanet has some form of life on it. That is, if the planet is in the habitable zone, the right distance from its sun so that its surface is not too hot and not too cold and could therefore have liquid water. These clues won't tell us how complex the life might turn out to be: It could be anything from algae to an advanced technological civilization.

Planets outside our own solar system may have evolved using an entirely different recipe for life from Earth's. Near one star, one set of life's building blocks might have developed in one way, while near a different star, the mixture might have been quite different. As one scientist puts it, we shouldn't expect "a twin of our own Earth" but should be

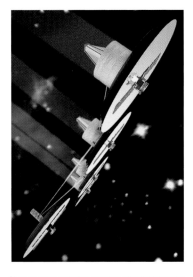

Using multiple telescopes that work together, the Terrestrial Planet Finder will search for Earthlike planets that may harbor life.

RAY JAYAWARDHANA

PROFESSOR OF

ASTRONOMY

UNIVERSITY OF

MICHIGAN

When he was a young boy, Ray Jayawardhana wanted to be "a pilot or an astronaut or something which just sounded really exciting." Then, when Ray turned fourteen, Halley's comet streaked across the night sky above his country, Sri Lanka. With a group of others, Ray traveled south from the capital city of Colombo, where he lived, to the seaside town of Matara, where they would have a better view of the comet. When he saw it, he was hooked.

With other students, Ray helped found the Young Astronomers Association. Its patron was the famous scientist and science fiction writer Sir Arthur C. Clarke, author of *2001, A Space Odyssey.* Clarke happens to live in Sri Lanka. Every year now when Ray returns to his country, he pays a visit to Arthur C. Clarke, who has become one of his mentors. Another was Cyril Ponnanperuma, a biochemist at NASA Ames Research Center who was science adviser to the president of Sri Lanka. Mentors are a great help to young science students, guiding them and encouraging them. Ray is pictured here in front of one of the Keck telescopes.

ready for the astronomical exploration of "a menagerie of wonderfully odd worlds." That means searching for life as we don't yet know it.

Much later in this century, many decades from now, when the technology catches up to the dream, we may be able to actually see some of these "wonderfully odd worlds" in outer space. The most complex and ambitious future mission, *Life Finder,* will have an array of telescopes too large to be connected to one another in space. They'll fly separately, in precise formation, like military jets at an air show, with a distance of 4,000 miles between the outermost telescopes in the array. If and when this space interferometer gets launched, *Life Finder* will be able to take actual high-resolution pictures of Earth-size planets around distant suns, pictures that may reveal atmospheres, oceans, and continents.

PART TWO

Life or Something Like It

IN A LABORATORY AT NASA AMES in Mountain View, California, Max Bernstein and Jason Dworkin check a complex machine bristling with tubes, valves, gauges, glass, and shiny metal. Gesturing toward the machine, Max says, "Here we prepare a little comet, or a bit of interstellar space."

The same chemicals we have on Earth are likely to be discovered on extra-solar planets. We think so because we observe these same elements in distant stars and galaxies. And certain chemicals—including oxygen, nitrogen, and methane— are part of the recipe for life. Or, at least, life as we know it.

Into their closed vacuum chamber, scientists Jason and Max put molecules like the ones found in interstellar clouds and in comets: water, methanol, ammonia, and carbon monoxide. The temperature in the chamber is just 15 degrees above absolute zero. "This is what it's like in these dark clouds that are out there in space," Max says, meaning the clouds that are the birthplace of new stars and planets. After the molecules freeze, Jason and Max expose the ice particles to ultraviolet radiation.

The result? Three amino acids have appeared—serine, glycine, and alanine. Amino acids are the molecules that come together to create proteins, and proteins are the building blocks of life.

Does this mean Jason and Max have created life?

Not quite.

Earth life may have
begun in a warm
primordial soup. Or, the
elements could have
arrived from frigid
outer space.

CHAPTER SIX

It's Elemental

Just what is life? Ask a dozen scientists and you may get a dozen answers that depend on whether they're biologists, chemists, physicists, geneticists, astronomers, paleontologists, oceanographers, or other kinds of scientists. But they'd probably all agree that a living thing is something that takes energy from the environment and uses it to grow and reproduce.

On Earth, all known organisms depend on water and have a carbon-based chemistry. They are built of proteins, which are made of amino acids. The instructions for building and operating the organism come from a molecule called deoxyribonucleic acid (DNA). The genetic code of every creature on Earth, from bacteria to whales, is written with the same base chemicals in the same molecule. These chemicals, in sequence, make up genes, which are pieces of DNA. Most genes contain the information for making a specific protein, which then plays its part in the building and running of the organism.

Comet Ikeya-Seki swept past Earth in 1965. Billions of years earlier, the comets that bombarded Earth could have carried the building blocks of life.

The molecules created in Max and Jason's experiment are not proteins and certainly not life, because a lot of steps have to be taken to lead from amino acids to living things. But they are building blocks of life, a good starting point for trying to figure out the process by which life is created.

Back in the 1950s, two scientists named Stanley L. Miller and Harold C. Urey combined chemicals in a warm broth in their laboratory. By discharging electricity into the broth to simulate lightning, they were able to create amino acids. They then theorized that life could have begun on Earth when the planet was home to wet, warm "primordial soup" struck frequently by lightning.

By contrast, Jason and Max's experiments show, they believe, that amino acids don't need a warm broth to form in, that they can be created in the frigid conditions of space.

Amino acids have been found in meteorites that have fallen to Earth. At first, astronomers thought that the amino acids in these meteorites came from inside our solar system. Max and Jason's results suggest that these amino acids might have formed in giant clouds of icy particles from beyond our solar system and then hitched rides on comets, meteorites, and asteroids that crashed onto Earth during our planet's first few billion years.

"Working in their laboratory, Max comments, "Our experiments suggest that amino acids should be everywhere, wherever there are stars and planets. Amino acids are literally raining down out of the sky, and if that's not a big deal, then I don't know what is."

JASON DWORKIN

ASTROPHYSICIST

NASA GODDARD SPACE

FLIGHT CENTER

MAX BERNSTEIN

RESEARCH SCIENTIST

SETI INSTITUTE AND

NASA AMES RESEARCH

CENTER

"Back in high school, our chemistry textbook described the scientific theory of the origins of life in terms of a 'primordial soup,'" Max Bernstein says. "The now famous Miller-Urey experiments, devised to test the primordial soup theory, showed how…biotic molecules might have arisen by cooking up a little Earth in a flask." By contrast, Max and Jason created a little outer space in a freezer. About life beginning in outer space, Max says, "It may not be that efficient, but a cloud 100 light-years across makes a pretty big beaker."

Lest you still think all scientists are terribly serious and do nothing but ponder the mysteries of the universe, Max and his colleague Jason Dworkin made a plug-in for a computer game called Escape Velocity. It carried this warning: "The galaxy is a dangerous place, and sudden death can come without warning from invading fleets. Use of strict play and an escape pod is noble, but foolish. You can then judge if the destruction of your ship was due to your own stupidity or the whim of a random and uncaring universe."

They spend their lunch discussing, Max says, "whether we might encounter a pathological species convinced that it must eliminate all other forms of life for its safety, or whether we might be that species."

Earth may have been seeded with amino acids not long after it formed. Jason adds, "And since new stars and planets are formed within the same clouds in which new amino acids are being created, this increases the odds that life also evolved in places other than Earth."

And that takes us back to the question—how did life really get started? How can all the bits and pieces fit together to become living organisms?

A New Form of Life

Craig Venter is trying to find out. Back in 1992, he founded the Institute for Genomic Research and set about sequencing the human genome. Genome sequencing is figuring out the order of the chemicals that make up an organism's DNA. Now, Craig has given himself an even harder challenge—to create a brand-new form of life, right here on Earth.

Organisms are made up of cells, and the smallest organisms are made up of just one cell. They want to engineer a new species of microorganism from scratch, to make a one-celled organism with the smallest number of genes it takes for a cell to become alive. If he succeeds, the organism will be different from any cell known on Earth.

An organism is an independent living being. A microorganism is an organism that can be detected only with a microscope; microbe means the same thing. Most of the evolution of life on this planet is an evolution of microbes. They are crucial in converting matter into energy—and vice versa. We live surrounded by microbes every day. They're in our guts, in our mouths, on our skin, in the air we breathe, in our backyards—and at the beach, where a teaspoon of surface water can contain about five million bacteria and 50 million viruses.

We don't pay attention to microbes. They're intimate strangers, a part of our biology that we ignore because we're unaware of them. As one scientist puts it, "Earth is the Planet of the Microbes. A visitor to Earth during most of its history would have been greeted only by microorganisms. You could scrape all the big stuff off this planet, and the biosphere wouldn't mind very much. It would go on existing as it did for three-plus billion years before the big stuff made its presence known." The oldest fossils, nearly 3.5 billion years old, are fossils of bacteria-like organisms.

The research team led by Craig and his colleague, a Nobel Prize winner named Hamilton Smith, will begin with a simple bacterium. They'll remove more than 200 of this particular organism's genes, leaving a hollowed-out cell membrane. Then they'll put together a minimum number of genes and put them into the nearly empty bacterium cell. If the new cell survives, it will have become a new and never-before-seen organism, a whole new example of life. As a first step, the team succeeded in splicing together segments of DNA to make a synthetic virus. But, Craig says, "The goal is to fundamentally understand the components of the most basic living cell, trying to see if we can define life based on first principles. These are the genes required for metabolism to produce energy, these are the ones required to make the cell wall work."

It will take a lot of experimenting for the researchers to figure out which combinations of genetic material will create a living organism. If the new cell begins to feed and reproduce, it will be considered alive. Cell division will let it grow into a colony of cells, if the experiment works. The cells in Craig's experiment will be delicate; they're not expected to be able to survive outside the laboratory. At least that's what Craig and Hamilton have promised—that if the cells should escape, they'll die.

Even if Craig's team succeeds in creating a new form of life, it will still be Earth life with the same basic DNA instructions. But what if life *beyond* Earth has an entirely different genetic code? Would we recognize it? How will we know how to search for something so strange to us? Craig's work may help determine how life began on Earth, but it could also help us understand whether life beyond Earth follows different rules of biology.

The Beginning of Life

At the SETI Institute headquarters in Mountain View, California, a hundred scientists, educators, and support staff work together to find answers leading to the discovery of life beyond Earth—not just Project Phoenix's search for intelligent, extraterrestrial life that might communicate with Earth, but any life, anywhere beyond Earth: microbial, multicelled, or of a totally mysterious form.

Christopher Chyba has always had an insatiable ambition to solve mysteries. After earning his college degree in the United States, he studied physics and philosophy at Cambridge University in England. During his last year at Cambridge, Chris would visit the bookstore, where he noticed himself gravitating toward the section on the origins of life—at least to the few books available on the topic at that time. What mystery could be greater than the question of how life began? "Maybe this is what I want to do next," Chris thought.

When he returned to the U.S., life's origins continued to fascinate him. Eventually Chris joined the SETI Institute. He now coordinates the work of more than a dozen researchers in the field called astrobiology. The term itself has a lot of meanings: the study of the chemical origin of life, of evolution, of planetary biology; the search for extraterrestrial life; and research to support human beings in space. Life in the Universe projects at the SETI Institute focus especially on how life might have begun, and where or if it might exist beyond the limits of Earth.

Located about a mile down the road from the SETI Institute is the sweeping NASA Ames Research Center, with its two runways, three aircraft hangars, and 3.5 million square feet of facilities that include the headquarters of NASA's Astrobiology Institute. Here, too, scientists are working to find life beyond Earth. Describing its goals, NASA astrobiologists state, "Humans have pondered for millennia whether other inhabitable worlds exist. Now, for the first time, they have an opportunity to look and see, plus the opportunity to learn, 'What is the future of life here on Earth and in space?'"

To determine the future, astrobiologists start by going back to the beginning. Microbial life may have begun not just on our own planet Earth but in other places, too, and that's what astrobiologists are looking for—some good solid evidence of where and how life started. Like the astronomers who hope to analyze wavelengths from extra-solar planets, astrobiologists start their search with the one absolute necessity for life as we know it—water.

Frozen water has been found in lots of places beyond Earth. However, *liquid* water is much harder to find, and that is what is required for life. Liquid water might possibly be found beneath the dry surface of Mars, and it may also exist in an ocean beneath the frozen surface of Jupiter's moon Europa. But neither of those places would be what we human beings think of as a livable environment. In

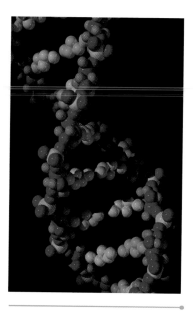

Two strands of DNA are held together in the shape of a double helix. DNA contains the genetic code for all living organisms except certain viruses.

addition to liquid water, a livable environment needs a source of energy (in Earth's case, that's usually sunlight) and a reasonable surface temperature.

Early Earth

NASA researcher David Des Marais calls himself a bio-geo-chemist, which adds up to astrobiologist. He says, "First we have to discover whether a planet is habitable, and after that we can look for the inhabitants. In the foreseeable future, we can send spacecraft to only a few planets to analyze them, and we can send spacecraft to even fewer places to bring something back and analyze it here." So to understand life, we must start by studying the only planet we really know—Earth.

When Earth formed about 4.5 billion years ago, it was continuously struck by comets and asteroids. But those comets and asteroids, as well as smaller debris, delivered water that helped give Earth its oceans.

Once the oceans formed, they would have protected any-thing deep within them from the damaging impacts on Earth's surface. Some scientists think that's where the first Earth life started—in the oceans. Like ocean-bottom dwellers today, bottom dwellers back when life began would have received energy not from the sun, but from chemicals deep within the seas. At least that's one of the possibilities that has been proposed. Nothing is known for certain about the ancient history of Earth. There are many theories, and many scientists are working diligently to examine the evidence, but it's a puzzle with pieces that don't fit perfectly.

Over hundreds of millions of years, the comet and asteroid bombardments began to taper off and the seas became calmer. Organisms rose to the surface, perhaps collecting in tide pools, where they did obtain energy from sunlight.

Bringing Color to the World

Some of Earth's earliest organisms were bacteria that combined in layers to form microbial mats. These mats first appeared in some shallow regions of the primitive seas. And then they spread. For billions of years they dominated Earth. Back when Earth was still a turbulent, wet place, microbial mats nearly covered the planet. Mats might have been the habitats for the first microorganisms that developed photosynthesis: the ability to capture the

Some 3.5 billion years ago on Earth, layers of simple bacteria and algae-like cells formed the first stromatolites—dome-shaped microbial structures in shallow ocean mud.

Microbial mats show many layers. For billions of years, microbial mats dominated Earth life, and they're still thriving today.

energy of sunlight and transform it into chemical energy, giving off oxygen in the process. Essentially all of the oxygen in our atmosphere was produced by photosynthesis.

Photosynthetic organisms brought color to the biological world. When you take a razor blade and cut down into a modern microbial mat, you can see the photosynthetic layers: orange and pink and purple and green. David Des Marais and other scientists at NASA's Astrobiology Institute are studying these communities of organisms that grow around hot springs in places like Yellowstone National Park, and in tidal pools alongside oceans. "That's our major research effort now," he says, "to find out what microbes live in these microbial communities and to learn how they work together."

If astrobiologists can understand how microbial mats work and how they evolved, it will help them identify and recognize microscopic life on other planets and in other solar systems. That's why, on the roof of the NASA Ames building where Dave's office is located, there's a small greenhouse filled with dozens of seawater containers holding filmlike, layered specimens of different-colored microbial mats. These thin mats, made of bacteria, are quite tough—they'd be able to survive an atmosphere like the ones on some extrasolar planets.

There's no question that the cells in Dr. Des Marais's microbial mats are alive. They do everything living organisms are supposed to do: use energy, take in nutrients, expel wastes, grow, reproduce, and die.

The reason the colors of the mats vary is that each layer uses a slightly different wavelength of light for photosynthesis. In years to come, when the *Terrestrial Planet Finder* is launched and its infrared cameras capture light from planets beyond our solar system, they'll check its wavelength patterns for possible matches to Earth's microbial mats and the chemical compounds they produce.

CHAPTER SEVEN

One Extreme to Another

We know that extrasolar planets might be boiling hot or colder than freezing. They might have no atmosphere, or they might have acid clouds. They might have little or no oxygen. They could be bombarded by damaging cosmic rays. As it turns out, there are places on Earth exactly like that, with severe, harsh, inhospitable conditions. It's in these places that scientists are searching for the kind of life that might be found in similar conditions on distant planets. More and more often, they find organisms that live where no one would have thought anything could survive at all. These Earth organisms are called extremophiles, meaning lovers of extreme environments.

On Earth, live organisms have been found in the driest, hottest deserts, on Earth's deepest seafloor, and on the highest mountain peaks. In certain places they're saturated by ultraviolet radiation. Some can survive in water that's hotter than boiling temperature, in deeply frozen ice-covered lakes, or in salt solutions that would

Grand Prismatic Spring in Yellowstone National Park is scalding hot, but it is home to millions of organisms called extremophiles.

pickle most creatures. Much of Earth is an extreme environment to humans, but for microbes, this is still the Goldilocks zone.

As an example, in Lake Vida in Antarctica, where the temperature can drop to minus 58 degrees Fahrenheit (minus 50 degrees Celsius), scientists drilled an ice core containing several layers of microbes that had clustered into mats. For 2,800 years, those microbes stayed frozen under 39 feet (12 meters) of ice. It's hard to imagine a more extreme environment. Yet when the ice core was thawed, the frozen microbes came to life. Microbes even older than that may exist deeper in the ice sheet that still seals the lake or in the highly salty water beneath the ice. If they do exist there, they would have to get their energy from chemicals in the water, because for thousands of years, they've had no contact with sunlight.

Under 39 feet of Antarctic ice, microbes have stayed alive for 2,800 years. That's extreme!

Witch's Cauldrons

Astrobiologists David Des Marais and Lynn Rothschild study extremophiles. Lynn has looked at microbial mats in Baja California in a salt pond three times saltier than the ocean and at organisms inside boiling geysers at Yellowstone National Park. She says, "Yellowstone has bubbling acid hot springs that would make a witch's cauldron seem benign. And yet they teem with life." The organisms they teem with are called thermoacidophiles—"thermo" for "hot" plus "acid" plus "philes" meaning "lovers." They're probably related to the first organisms that lived on Earth more than three billion years ago.

LYNN ROTHSCHILD

EVOLUTIONARY

BIOLOGIST

NASA AMES

RESEARCH CENTER

When she was in third grade, Lynn Rothschild looked through a microscope and saw a single-celled creature called an amoeba. From that moment on, she knew she wanted to study the tiny organisms called protists (protozoans, algae, and some fungi). What's so fascinating about protists? Lynn answers, "Protists are neat! They've got personality. I will admit, my husband works on bacteria, and I'm sure it's very nice to work on bacteria. But they have no personality, let's face it. You look through a microscope, and these protists are running around, and you've got this fantastic little world that is probably better than anything Steven Spielberg can think of."

From Yale University to Indiana University to Brown University, where she earned her Ph.D., Lynn's enthusiasm for protists has stayed as strong as it was in the third grade. She calls herself "a poster person for astrobiology." Today, at NASA, Lynn's research focuses on the evolution and ecology of...protists!

Today they thrive in springs that are not just hot, but boiling. The many brilliant colors in Yellowstone are caused by all the many different organisms living and growing the hot springs.

Lynn and her husband, Rocco Mancinelli, work together, but he works with bacteria, and she studies protists—organisms that include protozoa, algae, and some fungi.

Lynn and Rocco sometimes take their son, Kyle, with them on field trips to Yellowstone, where they've found pink-colored organisms alive and well in Octopus Springs. Hot springs are good places to preserve microbes. In a microbial mat found there, organisms on top use sunlight for photosynthesis, but as the mats grow thicker, they block sunlight from the cells underneath. These cells are then replaced by bacteria that can survive in dimmer light, and as the layers grow more numerous, the cells at the bottom adapt to live without photosynthesis.

Lynn has also examined what others call "scum" or "slime." Those may sound like insults, but they're valid scientific terms. Biological slime is spelled SLiME (that's capital S and L, small i, capital M and E). It stands for Subsurface Lithoautotrophic Microbial Ecosystem. Because SLiME organisms live deep in the Earth, they don't get energy from sunlight. Instead, these extremophiles absorb chemical energy from rocks. That's called "chemosynthesis." They also get nutrients such as carbon, hydrogen, nitrogen, and phosphorus, and use them to make DNA and proteins.

Delving deep into the Earth in Washington State, scientists found a SLiME community living more than 3,300 feet (1,000 meters) beneath the surface. Another group of microbes was found in solid lava more than a mile (1.6 kilometers) underground. Like some of their extremophile cousins, these organisms extract hydrogen and carbon from solid rock and water and use them as nutrients.

The deeper into the Earth organisms live—and they've been found nearly two miles down—the more extreme the environments become. At depths like that, the microbial colonies become fewer and older. Some may be several million years old. When the microbes can't find enough nutrients, they can shrink to a thousandth of their normal size. Because they're starving, they hardly reproduce at all—maybe once in a century. But they're still alive.

Finding the Unexpected

Scientists never stop looking for life. An early Nobel Prize winner named Albert Szent-Gyorgyi said, "Life is a wondrous phenomenon." He added, "Discovery is seeing what everybody else has seen, and thinking what nobody else has thought. Very often when you look for one thing, you find something else."

That's what happened to deep-sea biologist Cindy Lee Van Dover—she found the unexpected. According to Cindy, if scientists want to learn how life began, they'd be wise to study the deepest oceans. Most of the processes that formed Earth's surface, Cindy believes, are still taking place, right now, somewhere on the seafloor. She calls it "the largest and least known wilderness on our planet," commenting, "We know more about the surface of Mars and Venus and the back side of the moon than we know about the seafloor."

After graduate school, Cindy joined the group that operated the deep-diving submersible *Alvin*, the first deep-sea sub that could carry passengers, usually a pilot and two observers. Being an observer inside *Alvin* was wonderful, but Cindy realized that what she really wanted, more than anything else in her life, was to *pilot* the tiny, three-person vessel. That was not going to be easy.

In Love with ALVIN

One of the big problems involved living quarters. All the men in the training group bunked together. "Only the senior pilots got the luxury to have a room of their own," Cindy says. "The group didn't want to give up a berth to a scientist, let alone a woman," and Cindy was both. "Some of the big things I've done have been because

CINDY LEE VAN DOVER

OCEANOGRAPHER

COLLEGE OF

WILLIAM AND MARY

When she was a child, Cindy Lee Van Dover lived in Eatontown, New Jersey, five miles from the Atlantic Ocean. She wanted to have a workbench like her brothers had, and her own special tree to climb, but in her family "boys were expected to do boy things and girls were expected to do girl things." She did, though, get to spend every summer day at the beach. That was the beginning of her life-long love for the ocean and everything in it.

"My mom taught me to love nature, my dad taught me to love technology," Cindy says. "My biology teachers taught me well, and I had the privilege of working in a marine research lab during two of my high school summers. The scientists there were wonderful, and I wanted to grow up to be like them."

Today, those scientists probably wish they could be just like Cindy.

somebody didn't think I could do it," she admits, and so she refused to give up her quest. As she waited for her opportunity, she studied the sub.

Alvin can dive to almost 15,000 feet because it has been built to stand the crushing pressure of the deepest oceans. Some 23 feet long, weighing 19 tons, *Alvin* usually stays submerged for about 8 hours—1.5 hours to reach the desired depth, 5 hours for researchers to study the seafloor, and another 1.5 hours to get back to the surface. In an emergency, *Alvin's* life-support system would work for up to 72 hours, keeping the crew safe until rescue arrived. Mounted on the front are outside lights to illuminate the pitch-dark ocean, plus cameras and manipulator arms to pick up specimens from the ocean floor. Later they will be examined in a laboratory. Altogether, *Alvin* is a pretty exciting vessel.

"When the sub was on deck [of the ship that carried *Alvin* to the places it would explore]," Cindy says, "I would work inside her, and with my eyes shut, reach out to touch a specific one of the hundreds of toggle switches to learn their location by heart." At night Cindy pored over blueprints and safety specifications, memorizing emergency procedures. "*Alvin* dreams filled my nights," she remembers, "just as *Alvin* filled my days."

She kept applying for the training program, and her perseverance paid off. In 1990, Cindy Lee Van Dover, Ph.D., became the only woman and the first scientist ever to have completed the difficult training required to pilot a submersible. Over the next few years, she made more than a hundred dives, 48 of them as pilot in command.

Heat Lovers

Just as there are geysers in Yellowstone, there are also geysers at the bottom of the ocean. They're hard to find because they're hundreds of feet deep in water that light doesn't penetrate. These hydrothermal vents happen when magma, or hot lava, from deep inside Earth pushes up and breaks through the seafloor, spewing superheated columns of water full of mineral fragments. Also called black smokers, the vents are home to extremophiles with the scientific name of "thermophiles," meaning heat lovers.

Thermophiles at vents get their energy from chemical reactions rather than from photosynthesis. Bacteria have adapted themselves to live on the dissolved metals and other chemicals borne up in the eruptions from beneath the seafloor. Other sea creatures, such as mussels, eat the bacteria.

Cindy's first big discovery concerned a species of shrimp, *Rimicaris exoculata,* that lived around a vent. The shrimp had what looked like oval eyes—on their backs! When Cindy brought several of these shrimp to the surface and examined them, she found that the markings on their backs actually *were* eyes! But what could the shrimp see in the black depths of the ocean where no light penetrates? Because the shrimp cluster around superheated black smokers, Cindy and her colleagues speculated that they might get their visual signals from the infrared (heat) range

Seen through *Alvin*'s porthole, the manipulator arm reaches for samples at this black smoker—a hydrothermal vent on the ocean floor.

of the spectrum rather than from visible light because hot objects give off infrared waves. That was the first theory. Then things got really amazing.

On later dives to the seafloor, Cindy explored the 664° Fahrenheit (351° Celsius) black smoker named the Snake Pit. Using an instrument with a device that detects long-wavelength light that human eyes can't see, they discovered a pale glow. At the bottom of the ocean, where the sun can never shine, the instrument found light.

All marine biologists understand bioluminescence, the

light emitted by certain sea creatures and by fireflies and some mushrooms on land. This light at the vent was definitely not bioluminescence. So what was it? Cindy and her colleagues are trying to solve the mystery, because this light source might be what *Rimicaris* uses its eyes to see and because it could be another clue to life's chances on a faraway planet. That's the joy of science—to stumble upon an intriguing mystery and then try to solve it, no matter how long it might take.

However, science can be filled with disappointment as well as triumph—in fact, there are often more disappointments than triumphs. One big problem is finding money to pay for research. Scientists do this by writing grant proposals—explaining what their research involves, why it's important, and how much it will cost. They submit these proposals to the government, to science foundations, or to corporations that might be willing to finance certain kinds of research. Chris Chyba, the head of the Center for the Study of Life in the Universe at the SETI Institute, says many scientists spend three-quarters of their time working on their projects and another quarter trying to get money to fund their projects. In eras of economic downturn, research money becomes even harder to come by.

Then there's the competition to be the first to discover something. Ray Jayawardhana was frustrated when the sky turned cloudy over the Keck telescopes in Hawaii because he lost a night of observing. Each night lost meant that somewhere another astronomer might be forging ahead in the same quest to discover how planets form. Committees, usually including other scientists, have to make decisions about who gets to use telescopes and when, just as they must decide who gets money for research.

For seven years, Cindy Lee Van Dover and 34 other scientists tried to win funding for a trip to explore the floor of the Indian Ocean, to search for hydrothermal vents and new life around them. Twice their proposal was turned down by the National Science Foundation (NSF). When the proposal was finally accepted, the NSF gave them $400,000—but the real cost of the six-week trip would be a million and a half dollars. That meant the researchers would have to work without pay. They agreed.

The expedition to the Indian Ocean didn't use *Alvin*; instead the crew explored with *Jason*, a 2,200-pound (1,000-kg) robot about the size of a Volkswagen Beetle. *Jason* is tethered to a research ship by long cables that transmit video images to the researchers on board. To keep *Jason* from swaying back and forth underwater like a swing, the robot has to hang from a steel frame named Medea. A specially made elevator carries specimens from the ocean floor to the ship.

Shortly before the expedition was to begin, a Japanese team located the first hydrothermal vent in the Indian Ocean, beating Cindy and her team to the discovery. And that was just the beginning. Other frustrations followed.

A storm blew up, raising 15- and 20-foot-high (4.5- and 6-meter-high) waves that made it impossible for the team to bring up the elevator holding specimens. The ship took another direction until the waters calmed, then returned for the elevator, which was carrying $100,000 worth of equipment. But the elevator was gone, blown away by the storm. Not only was it lost, but a great deal of time was lost also, days the team could have spent searching for new hydrothermal vents. When they finally found a promising research site, they had only six hours left to explore it before the ship needed to return to its port.

Yet there were triumphs, too. They discovered shrimp around the vents in the Indian Ocean that were so much like *Rimicaris exoculata*, the shrimp Cindy had discovered in the Atlantic with *Alvin*, that they might be the same species. If that's true, how did the species travel 10,000 miles to appear in both the North Atlantic and the Indian Ocean? That's a new and intriguing question for marine biologists to try to answer.

Cindy's enthusiasm stays high. She says, "When I was young, I thought all the world was known, the list of explorers complete. Not true. There are oceans to be explored, on our planet and elsewhere." They're worth investigating because, "Life might have evolved at deep-sea vents. Our very origins may be linked to them."

CHAPTER EIGHT

Earth to Mars

Three and three-quarter miles doesn't seem like much of a distance—unless it's straight up. While Cindy Lee Van Dover studies extremophiles at the bottom of the ocean, Nathalie Cabrol studies them in the highest lake in the world. The lake doesn't have a name. It's 19,680 feet (6,000 meters) high, located in a crater on a volcanic peak called Licancabur in the Atacama Desert, on the border of Chile and Bolivia, in South America. "The volcano's dormant now. It hasn't been active for at least 500 years, and we hope it's going to stay this way!" Nathalie mentions, laughing.

Some 500 years ago, the Inca would climb to the nameless lake, hold celebrations, and set fires to send messages from one peak to another. Nathalie says, "The Incas were going there to try to understand better the secrets of nature and whatever god of nature was there, and to understand their place in the universe and the cosmos. And we are doing exactly the same."

Near the top of Licancabur's 19,730-foot peak, Nathalie Cabrol and graduate student David Fike pause for a breath of the thin air.

There near the top of the world, the lake is in the middle of a desert. Only a few centimeters of rain or snow reach its surface in a year. Most of the time, the lake is frozen over, and even when it isn't frozen, its water stays cold. At that elevation, atmospheric pressure is about half of what it is at sea level, and the oxygen content of the air is low, making it hard for people to breathe even when they're standing still. Because of the altitude, the lake gets bombarded with very high levels of ultraviolet radiation. This is an extreme environment.

Yet, the waters hold life. Extremophiles have adapted to the harsh conditions in that nameless lake at the top of the world. Nathalie says, "Since it's very isolated, we might run into the case of development of new species because they've been so long in isolation. Isolation is a wonderful tool for evolution."

Nathalie Cabrol and her husband, Edmond Grin, share an office in a building at the NASA Ames Research Center. They're geologists who like to climb mountains, a good skill to have when you're studying extremophiles at the top of one. "One of our great motivations to go to this altitude, breathe so little air, sleep in the cold, and be exposed to harmful UV [ultraviolet radiation]," Nathalie says, "is because we want to learn more about...Mars! And about life on early Earth, when no ozone layer was there yet to protect the life bombarded by high UV radiation."

She explains, "Here in Chile and Bolivia, it's all the same story, you see? Whe you think of Mars, you think of lakes on Mars that are dry now. You think also in terms of

NATHALIE CABROL
PLANETARY GEOLOGIST
SETI INSTITUTE
AND NASA AMES
RESEARCH CENTER

"I grew up near Paris, 25 kilometers west in what is called the 'green belt' of Paris, with parks and forests. My childhood was spent between my parents and grand-parents, and holidays with my cousin playing on the shores of the Mediterranean.

"It seems that I never wanted to do anything other than what I am doing today. At five, I was spending my summer nights watching the sky and the stars. During the day, I was playing with shiny pebbles in the lake where we spent our vacations in Italy or with the sand on the beach. One of my grandmas told me years later, 'When you were walking, you were never looking in front of you. You always looked at the stars or at the rocks.'

"I was born with this in me. The cosmos and the planets fascinated me. I loved nature very early and, as an only child spending many hours alone, I probably developed lots of curiosity and capacity to dream. I was never afraid to speak my mind when I thought I was right. I did not care if people thought I was a day-dreamer. I dreamed so hard that I made my dream become a reality. That's the secret—dreaming can make it all come true."

a planet that has a low oxygen, high UV environment and all sorts of nasty stuff going on. So what's driving me up onto that mountain is that we have a thinner ozone layer, maximum radiation, an atmosphere that's about half the atmosphere at sea level, and a lake that's covered by ice a significant amount of the year. Best of all, life is thriving in conditions that relate very much to Mars three and a half billion years ago. So this is why I go there."

It doesn't take long in geological time for life to appear on a planet if conditions are right. Earth was probably inhabited by microbes 600 million to 900 million years after its formation. Planets with habitable windows early in their history, like Mars, could have evolved life too, even if it didn't get very far before conditions became too cold and too dry to support it.

As a planetary geologist, Nathalie has spent countless hours poring over hundreds of pictures of the Martian surface, studying images taken by the Viking landers in the 1970s, and much later, by the two orbiters *Mars Odyssey* and *Mars Global Surveyor.*

In 2001, scientists were asked to suggest landing sites for twin robotic rovers that would land on the surface of Mars in 2004. To qualify, a site had to be near the equator, low in elevation, not too steep, not too rocky, and not too dusty. Nathalie proposed the dry Martian lake bed called Gusev. She thought the Gusev crater would be a great place for a rover to land because it's wide and has a dry riverbed going right into it. That indicates it could once have held a water-filled lake.

In addition to Nathalie's suggested site, 185 others were proposed by scientists who speculated on where Martian life might have existed. When the final two sites were chosen, Gusev was one of them. Then in June of 2003, secure on Delta rockets, the two Mars Exploration Rovers were launched from Cape Canaveral to make the long journey to Mars.

It isn't easy to get to Mars. Of 30 Earth-to-Mars mission attempts since the 1970s, two out of three have ended in failure. Edward Weiler, NASA's Chief of Space Sciences, calls Mars "a death planet." All the failed missions carried the hopes and dreams of dedicated scientists, not just in the U.S., but all over the world. In 1999, NASA lost two Mars-bound spacecraft—one of them, the *Mars Polar Lander,* crashed onto the red planet. In December 2003, a

Japanese space probe named *Nozoni* flew off course and had to be abandoned. Next a British lander called *Beagle 2*, scheduled to reach the Martian surface on Christmas Day 2003, never called home. No one knows what became of it.

In a fiery entry on January 3, 2004, *Spirit* streaked through the Martian atmosphere at 12,000 miles per hour. Its parachute snapped open to slow its fall. Airbags inflated, rockets fired to further reduce its speed, and then *Spirit* hit. It bounced—30 feet high! After bouncing again and again, it rolled to a stop right where it was supposed to be, in the middle of Gusev crater. After seven months and a flight of 303 million miles, *Spirit* had hit the bull's-eye.

At Jet Propulsion Laboratory (JPL) in Pasadena, California, scientists who had worked for years to achieve this triumphant landing couldn't stop cheering. Within hours *Spirit* started sending pictures of Gusev's red dirt and rocks back to Earth. To Nathalie, Gusev crater looked "simply beautiful!"

Twelve days after landing, *Spirit* rolled off its platform and headed for a rock the JPL team had christened Adirondack. "Rocks are collections of minerals," explains David Des Marais. "If you find minerals that form in water, you know they were formed under conditions in which life might have lived. That's why we get excited about rocks." An analysis of Gusev's soil and rocks show it could have come from volcanoes like Licancabur.

Then, in a perfect landing on January 24, *Opportunity* reached Meridiani Planum on Mars and sent back pictures of dark red-gray soil with slabs of lighter bedrock that

If Gusev crater might once have held a lake, why is it now dry, dusty, and rock-strewn? Where did the water go?

looked quite unlike the terrain in Gusev crater. Some 6,600 miles (10,500 kilometers) distant from *Spirit* on the other side of the planet, *Opportunity* had found a whole distinct landscape.

Using their mechanical arms to sample the ground beneath their wheels, drilling rock surfaces to learn what they're made of, taking pictures nonstop with five separate cameras each, the rovers sent back data nearly nonstop from Mars to Earth. NASA scientists received the data, examined it, and analyzed it.

Weeks later, at the beginning of March 2004, the world received the electrifying news—Mars once had liquid water! The evidence? For one, a rock drilled by *Opportunity* contains sulfate salts and other chemicals that can only be formed by the evaporation of liquid water. There are two ways the sulfate salts could have formed. In the first scenario, an eruption of volcanic ash could have built up layers of finely grained rock. Later, groundwater from beneath the surface could have percolated up through the layers to deposit the salts. The second possibility is that a surface pool or lake or a salty sea evaporated over time, leaving behind high concentrations of sulfate salts.

We know that on Earth certain organisms use sulfate as an energy source, so these deposits may indicate that life existed on Mars. Steve Squyres, NASA's lead investigator on the Mars Rover project, said, "The [Martian] ground would have been suitable for life. That doesn't mean life was there. We don't know that." We don't know, either, the depth of the Martian water or how long it was there or the climate of Mars at that time. But everywhere that we have liquid water here on Earth, we have life. And we now know that on Meridiani Planum on Mars a habitable environment once existed.

Hundreds of questions remain. The best way to answer them will be to bring some samples of Mars rocks back to Earth in a return mission that's already being planned for sometime in the next decade. We need all the evidence we can gather because we want to send humans to Mars.

Obeying instructions from Earth, *Spirit* examines a rock for clues about the ancient Martian climate.

CHAPTER NINE

Jupiter's Icy Moons

Although the planet hunters are searching for signs of life beyond our solar system, and the Project Phoenix team is scanning the skies for signals from faraway civilizations, neither group expects to actually visit whatever life it might find. But Mars is close enough to land on, and so are the icy moons of Jupiter.

Christopher Chyba hopes to see a lander reach Europa. One of Jupiter's 60 or more moons, Europa is a frozen sphere covered by ice that may be miles—even tens of miles—thick over what may be a liquid ocean. If there is water underneath all the ice, no sunlight could penetrate that far, so photosynthesis isn't likely to be happening on Europa. But as the study of extremophiles on Earth has proved, photosynthesis isn't a requirement for the existence of life.

When Galileo peered through his telescope in 1610 and discovered four moons orbiting Jupiter, he had no way of knowing that one of the moons, Europa, might have an

Europa's icy surface may hide a liquid ocean that holds life. In the future, a hydrobot could explore underneath the ice.

Unlike Earth, Jupiter has many moons. Europa is just one of them, but its possibilities for life intrigue astrobiologists.

ocean on it. In 1996, a spacecraft appropriately named *Galileo* took the first detailed pictures of Europa, which is about the size of Earth's moon. The pictures showed a huge, smooth ice ball with a lot of cracks and buckles and slabs of ice. Europa's relative smoothness seemed odd because the other moons of Jupiter and our own moon, as well, are pockmarked with craters from comet and meteor impacts. The few craters on Europa aren't very deep, and the ridges around them are not high, certainly not compared with the peaks and valleys of Mars.

This smoothness suggests to some planetary observers that Europa's icy surface covers a liquid ocean. They think that the surface sometimes cracks open and that when it does, liquid water and slush seep up to the surface, filling the craters and then freezing over, since the surface stays at minus 274 degrees Fahrenheit (minus 174 degrees Celsius).

Jupiter and two of its other moons, Io and Ganymede, exert a lot of gravitational pull on Europa, yanking it back and forth in its orbit. This gravitational pull distorts Europa's shape in a process called tidal flexing. The constant flexing causes friction, which creates heat that could keep the interior in a liquid state and cause the surface ice to crack.

If the ocean exists, the water that seeps up through the cracks just might contain microbes. During the eons when Europa and every other planet and moon in our solar system were bombarded by a rain of debris, tons of carbon and amino acids would have stuck to their surfaces. Comets could have carried other life-starting materials—

carbon, nitrogen, sulfur, phosphorus—to Europa, just as they did to Earth. There could be hydrothermal vents at the bottom of a Europan ocean, teeming with organisms that practice chemosynthesis.

As a planetary scientist, Chris Chyba was excited when NASA began planning a mission to send an orbiter to Europa to image the surface in great detail, and to bounce radar down through the ice to discover how far it extends. Later—much later—would come a robotic lander to skitter across the surface, maybe do a little melting of the ice, and then analyze what it found. Last, maybe (although far in the future), a "hydrobot"—a remotely controlled submarine—would melt all the way through the ice and explore Europa's ocean (if it has one).

All this would be difficult and incredibly expensive and would take years to engineer to make certain any organisms that might hitchhike from Earth on the lander or hydrobot would not contaminate Europan samples before they could be tested for life—or worse, put any oceanic system on Europa at risk. (Scientists at Lake Vida in Antarctica stopped drilling before they hit liquid water so they could figure out a way to reach the water without contaminating it.) Still, scientists would have plenty of time to figure out solutions to such problems.

Mostly, though, Mars continues to create the greatest excitement. Right after *Spirit* landed on the Martian soil, President George W. Bush proposed an ambitious new direction for the future of the space program. He said, "Probes, landers and other vehicles of this kind continue to prove their worth sending spectacular images and vast amounts of data back to Earth. Yet the human thirst for knowledge ultimately cannot be satisfied by even the most vivid pictures. We need to see and examine and touch for ourselves." We need, the president said, to send astronauts to the Moon and to Mars.

Getting There

Getting there will require an enormous outlay of money over the next two decades. NASA will have to shuffle items in its budget and cut certain programs. And these new manned expeditions won't be able to use current technology. To send humans on the long trip to Mars, NASA will need newer and faster spaceships. Luckily, they're already on the drawing board.

Project Prometheus, named after the Titan in Greek mythology who gave the gift of fire to humanity, will develop spacecraft that use nuclear power. Up to this time, space ships have been launched with liquid-fuel or solid-fuel rockets. When they get into space, their momentum carries them to where they're going. Once they arrive, small nuclear-powered generators may operate their equipment, but no nuclear-powered rockets have ever before launched a vehicle into space. Now it looks as if it's going to happen.

Nuclear fission engines will have many advantages. First, they'll let spacecraft fly three times faster than they do now. This could cut the time it takes to reach the edge of our solar system from 15 years to 5 years, and the time it

In fourth grade, Chris Chyba struggled with long division and multiplication. On television he saw scientists who seemed to have the ability to solve intriguing mysteries, but to be a scientist, you had to know math. His mother spent hours with him at the kitchen table helping him with his arithmetic, and he learned.

Chris's ninth-grade algebra class had 35 students. After each test, the teacher would hand back the papers, first to the students with the lowest grade, then working up through the ranks to the highest scorer. At the beginning of the year, Chris scored almost at the bottom. "It was awful," he remembers. But his teacher told him that if he moved up in the ranking, it wouldn't matter where he'd started, so again Chris determined to learn what he needed to know. "At 2 a.m. I'd be at the kitchen table studying," he says, "and my father would find me and say, 'Chris, why are you still up?'" Chris knew exactly why, and so did his parents.

He mastered algebra, and then in twelfth grade he began to study calculus. "When I was young, I didn't know what it meant, but it seemed to capture this sense of profound knowledge, this mysterious and exciting thing that I wanted to understand. When I did learn calculus, it opened up a whole new world." Like Ray Jayawardhana, as a boy Chris was intrigued by the books of Arthur C. Clarke. "They made you look at the world or think about a possibility you'd never thought about before," he says.

takes to get to Mars from seven months to two. In addition to speeding up a mission, nuclear propulsion would let a spacecraft carry a load a hundred times heavier than current rocket boosters can. With all of that extra strength, a spacecraft could carry more scientific instruments. In the case of *Jupiter's Icy Moons Orbiter*, that could mean radar to penetrate Europa's surface plus powerful data transmitting systems to send information back to Earth.

According to NASA's ambitious schedule, the next humans-to-the-Moon mission could take place as early as 2015. *Jupiter's Icy Moons Orbiter* may fly by 2016. As for the first human footprints on the planet Mars, NASA's vision is 2020.

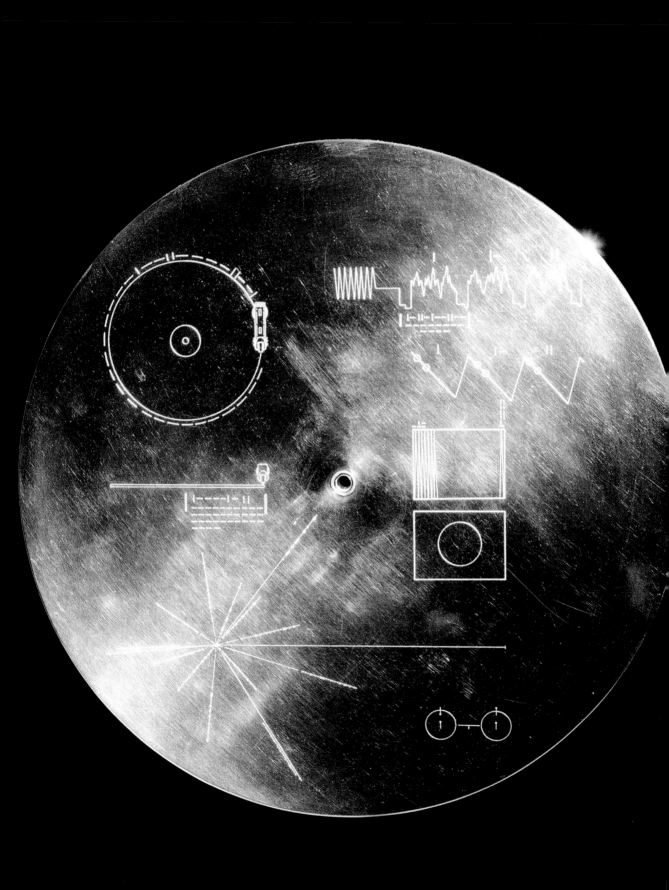

CHAPTER TEN

Talking to E.T.I.

While astrobiologists concentrate on the question "What is life?" there's another question that gets less attention—"What is intelligence?" Is it verbal ability? Parrots can be taught to speak. The ability to calculate? Sheepdogs can tell when a single sheep is missing from a flock—they'll hunt till they find it. The use of tools? Chimps crack open nuts with stones. The ability to adapt to an environment? Plants spread. The ability to communicate? Whales and dolphins do that.

If live microbes are discovered on Mars or Europa, we won't need to worry about communicating with them, because they won't have intelligence. But if an advanced technological civilization is discovered somewhere in the Milky Way galaxy, communication will be of the utmost importance. Suppose one night a signal from E.T.I. reaches the Allen Telescope Array. It won't be in English or Chinese or Russian or hippo or the language of any other living thing on Earth. But knowledge of the general rules of

The *Voyager* spacecraft carried a recorded message in 55 languages. The diagrams tell how to play it and also give information about the origin of the spacecraft. *Voyager* has reached the edge of our solar system.

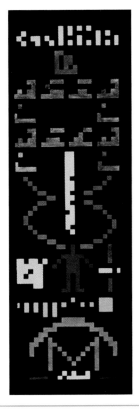

Sent to space in 1974, this signal shows the Arecibo telescope, our solar system, DNA, a human, and the biochemistry of life on Earth.

communication may help translate whatever message comes from the advanced civilization sending out the message.

The mathematical analysis of complex communication systems is called "Information Theory." At the SETI Institute, Laurance Doyle and his colleagues Brenda McCowan and Sean Hanser of the University of California at Davis were the first to apply it to dolphin whistles. They made a trip to Marine World, where, Laurance recalls, "That day the dolphins had their fun with me by tossing a ball to one side of the pool, where I ran around and got it, and after tossing it back they tossed it to the other side, where I ran around to get it, and they kept this up until I caught on to the notion that I was being run around on purpose. Looking at the natural smile on the profile of the dolphin who had been throwing the ball, it was difficult not to believe that I had just fallen for a dolphin practical joke. It is a well-known fact that dolphins have to think an experiment is fun or they won't do it."

Dolphins are considered by some to be second only to humans in intelligence. Researchers have already confirmed that dolphins communicate with one another by the sounds they make. Laurance and his colleagues decided to analyze those sounds to see if they created a pattern.

They had guidelines: some 60 years earlier, a language professor named George Zipf had made his students count all the letters in a lot of books written in English—not the words, but each individual letter. They figured out that *e* was used most (10.1 percent). It was followed by *t* (8 percent) and then *a*. They kept count all the way to *q* (0.1 percent).

When they drew a line through these numerical values on a graph, the line sloped downward at a 45-degree angle.

LAURANCE DOYLE
PLANETARY
ASTROPHYSICIST
SETI INSTITUTE

They tried the same thing with Chinese, which has more than 3,000 different characters, and got a 45-degree slope. Same for Russian, Arabic, and the other languages they tested. Calculating from the most common to the least common letters or symbols, the slope was always a 45-degree angle.

Using Zipf's Law as a guideline, Laurance and his colleagues decided to plot the different dolphin whistles. When the results were tallied, they found the same 45-degree slope as with human languages. Adult dolphins seem to have evolved a complex language. And so, perhaps, have whales. Laurance and his team are currently working with squirrel monkeys and elephant seals, as well—but not with the babies of any species. The babbling of human babies does not plot on that 45-degree Zipf slope, because it has no structure to it, and it turns out that immature birds, baby monkeys, and young dolphins also babble, making meaningless sounds.

Laurance and his colleagues have studied all those species, and now they're eager to analyze elephants, hippos, parrots, and bees. Bees? Not the sound of them, but the way bees communicate with a "waggle dance" when they've found honey. It tells the rest of the bees in the hive which direction to fly and how far.

"I got a map of the solar system when I was six," Laurance Doyle says. "I remember that distinctly, and I thought, 'That's it! Everything's not on Earth, so I'd better get studying the other things.'"

Laurance grew up on a dairy farm near the little California town of Cambria. The town was quiet and old-fashioned, with quaint narrow streets and old Victorian houses—not a promising setting for a precocious little boy who wanted to find out about "other things."

Laurance now recalls, "Nobody in my town knew what a logarithm was, and I wanted to know. I remember going around from house to house asking people."

What does all this have to do with the search for extra-terrestrial intelligence, the search for extraterrestrial communication? According to Laurance, E.T.I. signals will have to obey the rules of Information Theory to communicate, even if their languages don't have anything in common with any of the communication systems on Earth.

SETI Institute's Chris Chyba says, "If we detect an alien radio signal, we will at least have in common the physics and mathematics that made the signal possible. That would be a starting point." The spectra of distant stars seem to tell us that physics and chemistry are the same everywhere in the universe, and mathematical principles should be, well, universal.

Interstellar Messages

On four occasions, humans on Earth have sent messages into space, but they haven't received any answers. The most recent, sent in 1999 by Canadian scientists Yvan Dutil and Stephane Dumas, is pure mathematics. The message was beamed toward four nearby stars by the Evpatoria transmitter in Ukraine. Even Ivan admits that the message may not be understood. He says, "Many concepts are not translatable in math (at least at this point of our understanding). How do you describe the concepts of good and evil? What about love, or pain?"

That's why SETI Institute has its own resident psychologist. Doug Vakoch's business card reads, "Director of Interstellar Message Composition." It's a title for a scientist who spends his time wondering what will happen on

Earth if we do eventually make contact with extraterrestrial intelligence.

Doug says, "To create interstellar messages that have a realistic chance of being understood across interstellar distances, we need to identify some information shared by humans and extraterrestrials." One possibility, he says, is music. Music and mathematics have a lot of the same characteristics. "Even if E.T. is deaf, any of the civilizations we contact in the course of a SETI detection will be savvy about some of the building blocks of music. Concepts of frequency, amplitude, and duration are as basic to the construction of radio telescopes as they are to the composition of a symphony."

Then Doug suggests, "We're a young civilization, and perhaps we should be given the easy task, which is to listen. If we decide to transmit more messages, it will mean we're ready to engage in something that could take thousands of years, something that would be done for the benefit of someone other than ourselves. We need to start thinking about what we might contribute to the universe."

Jill Tarter says, "The Milky Way is vast. It's a pretty big cosmic haystack, and we're just pulling out a straw here and there. We're doing the best we can, and we'll do better as our technology improves, as we get cleverer, as we get the ability to look in the optical spectrum as well as the radio. But this is likely to be a generational endeavor. It may not be me, but my granddaughter who hears the first signal."

She adds, "If we do make contact, it will help us understand, as a species, our place in the universe. How we fit in.

Perhaps the search for E.T.I. will help us realize that here on planet Earth, all people are the same. We are human.

But I really hope that what will happen when we detect extraterrestrial intelligence, if we do, is that it will sink into people's minds that the E.T.s are not going to look like us, they're going to be fundamentally different than human because their evolution was totally independent. I hope it holds up a mirror so that we see ourselves, and we see them, and the result is that we forget about the differences among humans on Earth that we so often have trouble getting past."

And if we don't find E.T.I.? Jill answers, "There's an old *Pogo* cartoon that says it all: 'Either there's intelligent life out there, or there isn't. Either way, it's a pretty sobering thought.'"

MOST OF THE DIFFICULT WORDS in this book are defined in the the text. This glossary defines those that are not defined where they are first mentioned.

Amplitude: the maximum height of a wave

Anomaly: something different from a typical or normal condition

Antenna: a device for sending or receiving radio waves

Artifact: a feature not normally seen that may be the result of error

Atmosphere: the envelope of air surrounding the Earth; also the body of gases surrounding any planet or celestial body

Biosignature: an object or substance that could only have been created by life and could not have been created in the absence of life. Example: organic molecules

Channel: a band of radio frequencies assigned for one particular use

Cyborg: a living being who has mechanical or artificial parts or programs

Electromagnetic waves: waves that carry energy and travel at the speed of light. From the longest (weakest) to the shortest (most powerful), they include radio waves, microwaves, infrared waves, visible light, ultraviolet light, x-rays, and gamma rays.

Electron: an atomic particle that has a negative electric charge

Energy: the capacity of a physical system to do work

Image: a reproduction produced by capturing electromagnetic wavelengths given off or reflected by an object

Interference: signals, noises, etc., that obstruct reception of the signal being searched for by electronic equipment

Metabolism: the chemical processes in living organisms that turn food into growth and energy and eliminate waste materials

Molecule: a chemical made up of two or more atoms. The atoms in a molecule can be the same (an oxygen molecule has two oxygen atoms) or different (a water molecule has two hydrogen atoms and one oxygen atom). Biological molecules, such as proteins and DNA, can be made up of many thousands of atoms.

Pulsar: a small, dense neutron star that rotates fast and emits regular pulses of radiation

Random: unpredictable and irregular

Technological: able to create and use technology such as radios, telescopes, and other forms of communication in addition to other manufactured items

Transmission: transfer of data

Ultraviolet radiation: shorter in wavelength than visible radiation, the ultraviolet range of the Sun's rays that burns skin

Very Long Baseline Array: ten far-apart radio telescopes located from the Virgin Islands to Hawaii that work together as the world's largest full-time astronomical instrument

Very Long Baseline Interferometer: radio telescopes located all the way around the world. They can be linked together electronically to create an Earth-sized interferometer when needed. Eventually they may also be linked to a space telescope.

Between March 19, 2002, and February 28, 2004, the author interviewed the following people many times by phone, e-mail, in person, or all three: Tony Acevedo, Daniel Altschuler, Peter Backus, Max Bernstein, Paul Butler, Nathalie Cabrol, Chris Chyba, David Des Marais, Edna DeVore, Laurance Doyle, Jason Dworkin, Jane Fisher, Edmond Grin, Ray Jayawardhana, Heather Kowalski, Geoff Marcy, Randy McFarland, Diane Richards, Lynn Rothschild, Seth Shostak, Jill Tarter, Douglas Vakoch, and Cindy Lee Van Dover. In-person interviews took place at Arecibo, Puerto Rico; at SETI Headquarters, Mountain View, California; at NASA Ames Research Center, Moffett Field, California; at the American Astronomical Society Conference, Seattle, Washington; and in Boise, Idaho. Except as noted below, all quotes in this book come from those interviews.

• p. 14, Backus: "in a vast…" ("The Stars of Project Phoenix: The Best Are Not Always the Brightest." SETI Institute. April 17, 2003. http://seti.org); p. 16, Drake: "Our technology has…" (Quoted in a speech at the American Astronomical Society annual meeting, Seattle, January 2003.);• p. 16, Drake: "Our equipment today…" ("Search for Extraterrestrial Intelligence 40 Years Old." April 8, 2000. http://spaceflightnow.com/news/n0004/08seti40/); • p. 22, Shostak: "If an extraterrestrial…" ("Arecibo Diaries: Location Is Everything." SETI Institute. April 15, 2003. http://www.space.com/ searchforlife/shostak_arecibo_1_030415.html); • p. 24, Shostak: "There was the…" ("Arecibo Diaries: What It's All About." SETI Institute, March 21, 2002. http://www.space.com/searchforlife/ seti_diary4_020321.html; • p. 25, Shostak: "4505 has passed…" (Ibid.); • p. 27, Shostak: "thumb-size frogs…" (op cit, p. 22); • p. 27, Shostak: "We know that…" ("Arecibo Diaries: Is the Search Wishful Thinking or Hubris?" SETI Institute. April 24, 2003. http://www.space.com/searchforlife/shostak_arecibo_4_030424. html); • p. 30, Tarter: "Constructing individual small…" ("An Interferometer Is Born", SETI Institute. December 5, 2002. http://www.seti-inst.edu/about_us/info_for_media/back-grounders/inferometer_is_born.html); • p. 33, Marcy: "It's like watching…" ("Elite planet-hunter sleuths worlds for Cal" by Guy Ashley, *Contra Costa Times*, January 13, 2003. http:// www.bayarea.com/mld/cctimes/4934782.htm); • p. 34, Marcy: "The transit method…" (*Planet Hunters*, BBC, March 16, 2000. http://www.bbc.co.uk/science/horizon/1999/planethunters_script.. html); • p. 35, Marcy: "the tip of…" ("Hunting Planets Beyond," *Astronomy*, March 2000.); • p. 35, Marcy: "Every time you…" ("Hunt for Planets with Dr. Geoff Marcy at the W. M. Keck Observatory," Astronomical Society of the Pacific, January 2003. http://www.astrosociety.org/auction/faq.html#1); • p. 37, Jayawardhana: "Imaging a Jupiter-like…", "the reason people…", • p. 39, "If you can…" ("Cosmic Ray" by Nilika de Silva, *Sri Lanka Sunday Times*, January 28, 2001.); • p. 39, Jayawardhana: "The first one…" ("Imaging Exoplanets," by Robert Naeye, *Astronomy*, June 2003.); • p. 41, Jayawardhana: sidebar quotes (author interview and "Halley's Comet," *Sri Lanka Sunday Times*, January

28, 2001.); • p. 46, Bernstein: "Our experiments suggest…" ("NASA Scientists Create Amino Acids in Deep-Space-Like Environment," *NASA News*, March 27, 2002); • p. 46, Bernstein: "Amino acids are…" ("Seeds of Life Are Everywhere, NASA Researchers Say," by Robert Roy Britt, Space.com, March 27, 2002. http://www.space.com/scienceastronomy/generalscience/ amino_acids_020327.html); • p. 47, Sworkin: "Since new stars…" ("NASA Scientists Create Amino Acids in Deep-Space-Like Environment," *NASA News*, March 27, 2002.); • p. 47, Bernstein: "Back when I…" ("On the Extraterrestrial Origin of the Species: Molecules From Space and the Origins of Life," by Max Bernstein, *Strange Horizons*, June 4, 2001. http://www.strangehorizons.com/ 2001/20010604/origins_of_life.shtml); • p. 48, "Earth is the…" (David A. Stahl, Ph.D., University of Washington, Seattle, WA, in a speech at the American Astronomical Society annual meeting, January 2003.); • p. 49, Venter: "The goal is…" ("Scientists Planning to Make New Form of Life," by Justin Gillis, *The Washington Post*, Nov. 21, 2002.), "These are the genes…" ("Supermicrobe Man," by Douglas McGray, *Wired Magazine*, December 2002.), "There are so many…" ("Tinker, Tailor: Can Venter Stitch Together a Genome From Scratch?" by Carl Zimmer, *Science*, February 14, 2003.); • p. 51, "Humans have pondered…" (Posted, NASA Ames Research Center); • p. 58, Rothschild: "Yellowstone has bubbling…" ("Life in Extreme Environments: The Universe May Be More Habitable Than We Thought." http://www.spaceref.com/news/viewnews.html?id=462); • p. 59, Rothschild: sidebar ("Protists Have Personality." http:// www.accessexcellence.org/BF/bf05/rothschild/bf05b2.html); • p. 61, Szent-Gyorgyi: "Discovery is seeing…" ("The Scientist Speculates, 1962." http://www.dailycelebrations.com/063001.htm); • p. 61, Van Dover: "We know more…" (see Books: Van Dover, p. 4); "When the sub…" (see Books: Van Dover, p. 24); "When I was young…" (see Books: Van Dover, p. 1); • p. 62, Van Dover: sidebar (see Web Sites: Let's Talk With…); • p. 71, Cabrol: sidebar (author interview and http://extremeenvironment.com/2002.); • p. 75, Cabrol: "I find myself…", "I wish I could…" ("Tense Times as *Spirit* Closes In On Mars," by Leonard David. Space.com, January 2, 2004.http://www.space.com/missionlaunches/spirit_update_040102. html); • p. 76, Des Marais: "Rocks are collections…" (*Atlanta Journal Constitution*, Jan. 17, 2004.); • p. 79, Chyba: "I think that…" ("Looking for Life Beyond Earth." http://www.space.com/ searchforlife/astrobiology_special_010215-8.html); "The next few…" ("Jupiter's Moon Europa and the Rebirth of Exobiology" *Eberly College of Science News*, February 26, 2000.); • p. 86, Chyba: "If we detect…" ("SETI and the Search for Life," *Astrobiology News*, July 30, 2001.); • p. 86, Dutil: "Many concepts are…" http://library.thinkquest.org/C003763/pdf/interview01.pdf).

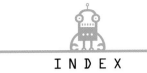

The page numbers in **bold** refer to illustrations.

SELECTED BIBLIOGRAPHY

BOOKS

Altschuler, Daniel R. *Children of the Stars: Our Origin, Evolution and Destiny.* Cambridge University Press. Cambridge, UK: 2002.

Haine, Peggy. *Arecibo Observatory.* Cornell University. Ithaca, NY: 2000.

Jackson, Ellen. *Looking for Life in the Universe.* Houghton Mifflin. New York: 2002.

Jayawardhana, Ray. *Star Factories: The Birth of Stars and Planets.* Raintree Steck-Vaughn. New York: 2001.

NASA. *Beyond Einstein: From the Big Bang to Black Holes.* NASA Office of Space Science. Washington, DC: 2003.

NASA. *Origins: Roadmap for the Office of Space Science Origins Theme.* Jet Propulsion Laboratory. Pasadena, CA: 2003.

Sagan, Carl. *Cosmos.* Random House. NY: 1980; 2002.

Shostak, Seth. *Sharing the Universe: Perspectives on Extraterrestrial Life.* Berkeley Hills Books. Berkeley, CA: 1998.

Skurzynski, Gloria. *Discover Mars.* National Geographic Society. Washington, DC: 1998.

Skurzynski, Gloria. *Waves, the Electromagnetic Universe.* National Geographic Society. Washington, DC: 1996.

Van Dover, Cindy Lee. *The Octopus's Garden: Hydrothermal Vents and Other Mysteries of the Deep Sea.* Addison-Wesley. New York: 1996.

WEBSITES

Arecibo Observatory: http://www.naic.edu/

Astrobiology: http://astrobiology.arc.nasa.gov

Astrobiology Magazine: http://www.astrobio.net/news/index.php

Astrobiology Missions:
http://astrobiology.arc.nasa.gov/missions/index.cfm

Astrobiology Web: http://www.astrobiology.com/

Astronomy Picture of the Day: http://antwrp.gsfc.nasa.gov/apod/

Geoff Marcy & Paul Butler: http://www.discover.com/issues/nov-03/features/discover-awards/spacescientist/

Jupiter Icy Moons Orbiter: http://www.jpl.nasa.gov/jimo/

Lake Vida:
http://www.campbellsci.co.uk/Applications/lake_vida_background.PDF

Let's Talk with Cindy Lee Van Dover: http://www.amnh.org/education/resources/rfl/web/dsv/dover.html

Licancabur Expedition: http://extremeenvironment.com/2003/

Mars Exploration Rovers Mission: http://marsrovers.jpl.nasa.gov/

NASA Ames Research Center: http://www.arc.nasa.gov/

NASA Origins Program: http://origins.jpl.nasa.gov

NASA Quest: http://quest.arc.nasa.gov/index.html

National Radio Astronomy Observatory: http://www.nrao.edu

Search for Extraterrestrial Intelligence, SETI Institute:
http://SETI.org

Voices: Christopher Chyba and Jill Tarter:
http://www.seti.org/seti_nai/voices.php

Voyager: http://voyager.jpl.nasa.gov/

Woods Hole Oceanographic Institute: http://www.whoi.edu/home/